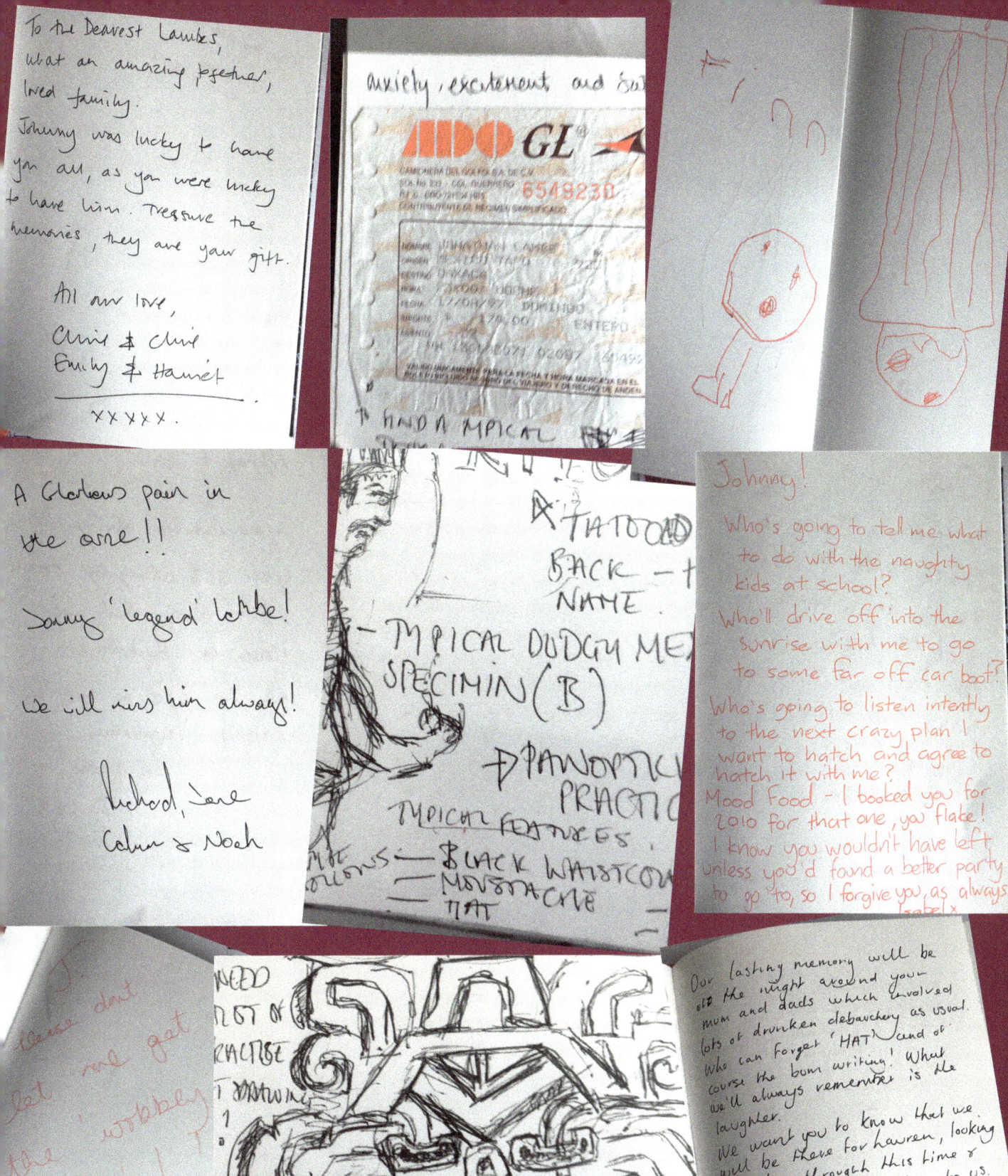

George's marvellous medicine

Love from Ruari

Johnny once asked me to elope with him to Paris. We ended up in Glasgow. That sort of sums him up really... glamorous, gritty, a rollercoaster of experiences and emotions from love to hate... and back again.

He was a light in my life, he taught me to be free, not to be afraid of anything, to chase my dreams. He made me who I am and I will never ever forget the wonderful times I had with him. He will live on in a million different ways and though I won't name ALL my children Johnny, I will never forget him.

Love to you all in these difficult times. Be sure that he is smiling down on all of us from some sunbeam....

lots of love, Kate xxxxx

My dear friend Johnny,

We had so much fun together at Manchester and we continued to party in London. So many special memories. I have been naughty pixies. I will miss you and miss your laughter.

All my love
Karen xxx

Jonny,
Man with a camera and a wonderful eye for detail, for this loss is heaven's gain, the sky will shine one star brighter. Shine bright! Shine forever

[signature] xxx
& Beth xxx

Johnny,
Never shall I forget your duet with Helen, at the front of the bus on the coach microphone!!! Total eclipse of the heart!!!

Bless you
Pete

BRITISH AIRWAYS
NAME OF PASSENGER
LAMBE/J MR
FROM LONDON LGW
TO MEXICO CITY
FLIGHT BA 2243 CLASS M DATE 14AUG TIME 1315
BOARDING TIME 1235 SEAT 53H
1 16 0

Johnnie

It was such a privilege knowing you and seeing you grow up to be such a handsome, funny and accomplished young man. What great times we had on those walks on the downs, even the time that you lost poor anold Josh.

Miss you and much love
Irene xxxx

Dear Jonny
You will never be forgotten. You always had a smile that would fill a room.
Missing you
Pamela

Hey Tomato man - don't ever forget me. Yours, Boy-boy (Marta) x

---

...and could we lend him a few pounds for his taxi waiting outside. Jonny invited in the dashing conman and we all gave him some cash + a drink .... and he then left whereupon we realised he'd also swiped a mobile phone.

JONNY →

the next day Johnny stumbled upon the thief in Dalston and spent an hour chasing around an estate while on the phone to the police .... all for a nokia 2210.

Johnny Lambe

Each X means a Million Kisses

A Memoir

By

Mona Lambe

Copyright © 2021 Mona Lambe

All rights reserved. No part of this publication may be reproduced or transmitted in any form or by any means, electronic or mechanical including photocopying, recording or any information storage or retrieval system, without prior permission in writing from the publishers.

The right of Mona Lambe to be identified as the author of this work has been asserted by her in accordance with the Copyright, Designs and Patents Act 1988

First published in the United Kingdom in 2021 by

Moyin Books

ISBN 978-0-9576015-1-2

Contents

Introduction 1977	1
Chapter 1 Coleraine 1988	14
Chapter 2 Brighton 1992	38
Chapter 3 Interrailing	43
Chapter 4 Manchester 1995	52
Chapter 5 Mexico 1997	68
Chapter 6 Johnny 1998–2007 by Mona Lambe	94
Chapter 7 London	97
Chapter 8 New York, New York 2001	102
Chapter 9 South America 2003	108
Chapter 10 London 2003	123
Chapter 11 A career develops 2004	127
Chapter 12 Une Periode de Calme (A period of calm)	132
Chapter 13 The End of Our World	147
Chapter 14 All Saints Church	150
Book of Memories	156
Who? Where? When	187
Postscript	195
Acknowledgements	198

Introduction

1977

I am never really sure as to whether my earliest memories are real or just a figment of my imagination.

Questions, questions, questions!

Did I bite the end of my dog's tail? Did I really have the dog's tail in my mouth and spit it out? Did the old drunken hippy who lived in the attic fall asleep on our rabbit and crush it to death? Did I get a stiffy as a baby every time the eighteen-year-old blonde girl next door came around to give me a bath? Did my bipolar cousin come around and build a log cabin in the garden? Did I turn up at one of my parents' dinner parties totally naked and covered with measles? Did I see a snake in the creek on the way back from watching ET at the drive-in? Is it a dream that my dad tripped and smashed my brother's head through a plate-glass window? And did I walk through Toronto crying because I missed Belfast?

One thing I know for sure: I loved Toby. He was my best friend. I showed him how my mum and dad zipped their sleeping bags together on camping holidays. We used to dress up, lock ourselves in the blue room and play strip poker. I remember Mum coming in and saying, "Why are all the clothes out of my wardrobe lying on the floor?" After the hurricane in October 1987, we found a porn magazine. The pages were stuck together, but when we pulled them apart we could see things we didn't understand but which we knew were important. We hid the magazine in a place that we alone knew: in the roots of a tree that had gone over in the storm. That night I told Mum and Dad about the magazine. It felt like a confession, but I didn't know what I was confessing to.

Mrs. I came to Balfour as a supply teacher, as Mrs N left because she'd had a nervous breakdown. Mrs I's hair was like a badger: black with a white stripe. I took charge of the 'Sack Mrs I Society'. We made posters and paraded outside the headmaster's office.

We did not get her fired, but during our political alliance we learnt the arts of snogging and smoking. Cigarettes were what we all wanted, and flat tops were the hairstyle statement of the day. P looked like a boy; she had one. I had one, and S, one of the French twins I played violin with, had one. Her twin, C, had floppy hair like a boy. S was the enemy. We would stand outside her house and howl like wolves or throw things at her bedroom window, just for a reaction of course. She lived next door to H and T, Japanese boys who had an early curfew.

At lunchtimes the bushes at the bottom of the field were the only place to be. This area was strictly forbidden, and patrolled, as there had been reports of strange men ...

A friend of Mum's called me '*un grand voyageur*' (a great traveller). This memoir is about some of the places I visited on my journey, from its beginning in Belfast to its end in London. What a rollercoaster ride! I wouldn't have missed it for the world.

I am Jonathan William Lambe, I was born on the 19th March 1977 in the Royal Maternity Hospital in Belfast. I am the third of four children and I was baptised in Rosemary Presbyterian Church Belfast.

I was happy living in Donegall Park Avenue. We could see Cave Hill from our back garden, with the apple orchard and log cabin. We often walked up to Belfast Castle on Sunday afternoons, looking for the stag. The path had a steep incline and was muddy. Dad pushed the youngest baby in the Pedigree pram up the hill, with the next one up sitting on top. When I was the baby it was Lauren and me being pushed, then when Nick came along it was Nick and me. Cheryl, our navigator, always ran ahead to find all the potholes and, of course, be the first to see the castle and see how many of the nine cats she could find.

I went to nursery school in St Peter's Church. Two friends live nearby, and they also went to St Peter's. One boy, Simon, had a Spanish mum, and the other, Matthew, had a journalist dad. We were destined to lose contact with each other, as the primary schools we were to go to were not integrated like St Peter's.

We had great times in Ireland with the cousins on Uncle Roy's farm, especially riding Candy.

Christening Shawl crocheted by Mona for all her babies

Johnny riding Candy with Uan and Mum

Playing 'The Entertainer' by Scott Joplin in the Europa Hotel, Belfast

The Billingsleys

Dad did not want to live with the bombs and bullets any more, after being in a hold-up in the Allied Irish Bank one day on his way home for lunch.

We moved to Canada. I was home-schooled for a year in Oakville, Ontario, as children didn't start school until six years old. Home-schooling was very informal: listening to stories, drawing—I even won a poster competition, but unfortunately they didn't return the poster to me—painting, singing songs to help learn numbers and the alphabet, learning to write my name, cooking, swimming lessons, gymnastics club, going to the library to choose new books and do a children's computer course, visiting Toronto, art classes, and concerts at the Ontario Place Centre, where we listened to Sonny Terry and the Chicago All-Stars Blues Band featuring Brownie McGhee. On one occasion, my sister walked down to the edge of the stage to get a photo of Kris Kristofferson in concert. As we left the concert in Ontario Place, we were all amazed to see KK's ginormous tour bus.

Glen Abbey Golf Course was behind our house in Oakville. In the summer we watched the golf, walked in the woods, kept an eye open for rattlers and spent many happy hours with the Kennedy children in the paddling pool or playing 'Who's Afraid of Mr Wolf?'.

Winter fun was snow-walking, sledging and ice-skating, not to forget trick-or-treating at Hallowe'en. We remember the sunny days of childhood; these were indeed halcyon days.

Picnic with Angela and the children before we departed to Canada

McCraney Street Gang Oakville, Ontario

Winter in Oakville

Niagara Falls, Ontario

While we were in Canada, the Falklands War broke out and Ireland won the Triple Crown. There was little coverage of the former in the media, but we were sorry to miss this big moment for Irish rugby.

In 1982, back in the UK, I started Balfour Primary School in September. The classroom was a bit of a shock to the system, as I was not used to large numbers. I felt a bit nervous as I went into the second year, as I was only five and a half years old.

Mrs Saunders was my favourite teacher ever. She 'got me', as the saying goes. "Johnny doesn't like to sit at his desk, so I just let him walk around with me. He is always quiet and polite and really interested in the other children's work. No trouble at all."

There was a lot of playground bullying. Mum's politically incorrect advice was, "If anyone punches you, just give them one good punch straight to the nose. You may get hurt, but they will remember it. Bullies are cowards, so don't be afraid."

I said, "We are not allowed to punch."

This problem was solved when Mum spoke to the teacher and arranged for me to walk alongside her in the playground. I think being given permission to retaliate and having playground support gave me confidence, and I had no more problems.

Johnny. Self-portrait at Balfour School

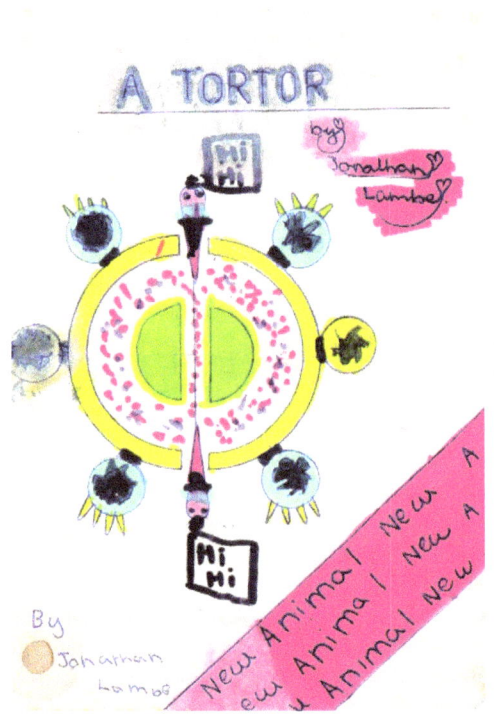

TORTOR by Johnny Lambe

Birthday card for Dad. 1st year at Balfour Infants

I enjoyed the sleepover parties, playing the violin at the Royal Albert Hall, walking home from school with friends and running around Stanmer Park. Toby (my 'bestie') and I toddled around at our ease, chatting happily as the others passed us by, but we did put on a bit of a sprint for the last twenty metres, just to impress the onlookers with our finishing skills!

Johnny and best friend Toby at Balfour

Birthday sleepover with Balfour Class

Johnny playing his violin at the Albert Hall

Sports Day at Balfour and London visit with the Hodeberts

During the summer holidays we went camping in France: Port Blanc in Brittany. Term ended a week early for us (Mum and Dad were accustomed to summer holidays beginning at the end of June). We packed up the car with all the camping gear: food and clothes, plus lots of soft toys in our pillow cases, unbeknown to Mum and Dad. We slept overnight on the boat, drove to the campsite and pitched the tents. Cheryl, who was a Girl Guide, had the two small tents up in a flash: one for Nick and her, and one for Lauren and me. The family called Lol and me 'The Rottweilers', as we were not morning people, and the question every morning was, "Who is going to waken the 'Rotties' today?"

The big tent for Mum and Dad was always a hassle, especially if there was wind and rain, so it was all hands on deck.

It is a municipal campsite at Port Blanc. Campers come from all over Europe: Dutch boys in their designer vans, and Germans with all the big-boys' toys—such as boats, bikes, enormous vans—and beautiful girls. We went for midnight swims (10 p.m. really) with the German family. Mum made hot chocolate with Fundador (Spanish Brandy) in it for the grown-ups. Big Bill from Yorkshire was a favourite. He had a three-legged stool, and each night he would choose a 'victim' who was generously plied with red wine and who never failed to topple off the stool, to the delight of the onlookers who knew what was afoot. Dad was one such victim. After his fall from grace, he was escorted 'home' and unceremoniously pushed into his tent by Dorit, where he collapsed face down on top of the sleeping bag. Big Bill's five-year-old son liked to join us on the beach for lunch. "Moonaa, can I have one of your butties?" he'd ask. "Ahhh likes them there butties."

Port Blanc with Maryvonne

Most evenings Dad would take us walking: sometimes into Dinard for ice-cream, hot dogs or *gaufres* (waffles), and often to walk around the headland at St Lunaire, passing the German bunkers and getting a little history lesson en route. St Lunaire is Dad's favourite walk, as he'd first done it when he was twelve years old. The walks were like an international school outing, with two Dutch boys, two German boys, a teenage Dutch boy and girl, and four Northern Irish children. Sometimes we were joined by our friends, the Stemp family ,from Brighton and the Billingsley family from Belfast.

Camping with the Dutch family at Port Blanc

Cheryl and Johnny, Port Blanc

Johnny with the Elephant at the Circus Valras Plage

We often walked around the ramparts at St Malo, but that wasn't quite as relaxing as the coastal walks, as we had to drive to St Malo, where it was nearly impossible to get a parking space. Once, we were window shopping in St Malo as it was getting dark and the lights were beginning to twinkle. A very tall man wearing a blonde wig, blue eye make-up, black stockings, a miniskirt and green nail polish came to the door of his shop as we were passing. I was mesmerised. We didn't talk about it; we just walked down to the harbour front and I sat for a cartoonist. That was July 1988.

Beside our campsite at Port Blanc there was an International Summer School where young people from all over the world came to learn to speak French. For three weeks we listened to them singing songs from *West Side Story*. Then the word got out: "*Spectacle ce soir a 21 heure, gratuit*—Show tonight at 9 p.m., free." Live theatre by moonlight in Brittany. We were transported by Bernstein's music to the world of the Sharks and the Jets. Sombre on the walk home, but youthful optimism took over and we entertained the other campers with strains of 'America', 'Tonight' and 'Somewhere'. What a night!

We became friends with two French families; however, their children weren't allowed to come on the walks. We were intrigued because their blind grandfather came on holiday with the family and they took it in turns to guide him to the shower block. We were invited to stay on their farm in Fougeres with Jean-Pierre, Georgette, Nolwenn and Soizic. One evening, during our stay, we all set out to visit the cousins: Maryvonne and Michel Peudenier and their three children. This was 'the night of the flying apple tart'. Jean Pierre set the tart on the roof of his car while he unlocked the driver's door. We were to follow behind, so we could see he'd forgotten to lift the tart off the roof. He took off at the rate of knots. It was a 'will it, won't it' situation. The tart stuck fast to the roof. We laughed and cheered all the way. Good old Jean-Pierre; he was going to get it there intact ... until the last bend before the cousins' house. The tart flew off the roof like a Frisbee. We were horrified. What would Georgette say? "*Pas de dessert ce soir*—No dessert this evening," was her only comment. She had, after all, lived with Jean-Pierre for a long time.

Caricature drawn at St. Malo 1988

Chapter 1

Coleraine

1988

In September 1988 I went to board at Coleraine Academical Institution (known as Coleraine Inst.)—an exciting new adventure, I hoped! We stayed on the farm with the cousins while preparing all the things necessary for boarding. What fun we had herding the cows and riding Candy. Jumping the fences Lorraine had set up was an exciting challenge. Mum enjoys riding and was easy to persuade, but Dad agreed reluctantly to have a go. Roma smacked Candy's rump to set her off. Fear took hold of Dad as he approached the first jump. Candy soared over the jump (about two feet high) without Dad, who'd abandoned the horse just in time, so came off sideways instead of head first. A good call, me thinks.

Next stop, the renowned school uniform shop, Moore's, in Coleraine. I enjoyed a 'spend up', and I was particularly pleased with the striped blazer.

***

I wrote lots of letters from Coleraine, mostly because I was so bored. At first boarding school was an exciting adventure. I raced off with my new friends to explore, just glancing briefly over my shoulder to say goodbye to Mum and Dad.

I had good and not-so-good teachers. Mr Cassells, the history teacher, was very good, as was the piano teacher, the tech teacher (Mr Edwards) and the PE teacher (Mr Graham). The RE teacher, Mr Foot, was 'desperate' (in NI speak that means woeful).

Most days after lessons I played badminton or went for a jog. I had table tennis lessons with a fifth-former, and we often went swimming in the evenings. The food was okay, but not as good as Mum's by far. When I was hungry I could go to the kitchen and they gave me some biscuits, fig rolls and a cup of tea. Time passed quite quickly, but I looked forward to the Hallowe'en holiday.

17 November 1988

    I'm back at school again after the half-term holiday, which used to be called the 'Potato Gathering' holiday, for obvious reasons. This week has gone very quickly. I've been working on my project and have finished the second chapter of 'Local Structures in Brighton'. I got an A+ in English and nine out of ten for story-writing—the highest in the class. All the rest were A's. Mr Cochrane (English) says I have improved a lot since the beginning of term and if I keep on improving, I'll do well in the exams. My French scores are averaging forty-seven out of fifty. The piano teacher got me loads of music: 'Fur Elise', 'Moonlight Sonata', 'Londonderry Air' and some rock 'n roll. I'm starting to like the piano teacher, and she is actually teaching me now—amazing. I'm allowed to stay in the classroom, no longer having to go into a little room to practise.

    All my love to Nick, Cheryl, Dad and you. I love you.

    From,

    Joni (son) (Chinese)

I'll write again and see you soon. Hope you like my story.

THE DAY DARYL BROKE THE SCALES

One day Daryl was homesick: so homesick that he cried and cried until we thought he'd never stop! When Daryl did stop crying, he started to eat and eat and eat. We thought he would explode. He ate out the whole of the tuckshop, and still he was hungry. He ran down to the ice-cream van and put his mouth under the ice-cream machine, pulling the huge lever. He ate enough of it to make fifty ice-creams. Then he was sick. He started to run again. He ran into town and went straight to Boots. Not for food; he headed straight for the scales. This now enormous boy jumped onto the scales and put in ten pence. Suddenly, a rumble came from below his feet. *CRASH*! The floor had fallen completely through. Daryl had broken the scales.

It was, of course, all a dream. I woke up and looked around. I was in maths class.

Johnny's drawing of Daryl Coleraine

Hi Mum (Hungry Eyes),

   I loved the way we went into the dining room and danced to *Dirty Dancing* music before we left for the airport. 'Hungry Eyes' is a favourite since Lol, Auntie Em and you went to see *Dirty Dancing* at the cinema.

   I am desperately missing you. I am miserable and hate it here, despite there being nothing wrong. I only got ten minutes in the pool on Monday night, which was very boring. I played rugby on Thursday—full back—and only got the ball twice, but thoroughly enjoyed it. I made a wooden mould for my fuse tester in technology and went into town for about half an hour. Mrs Foote came over in the middle of prep to see me. She took me over to her house and talked to me. That cheered me up a lot.

Triptych sketch 1. Mary had a little lamb

Triptych: Where is Mary

Landscape
Landscape with lake
Sheep in a meadow one black

Dear Mum

A boy in my class has invited me for the weekend. He lives on a farm nearby and is my best friend. Piano and violin lessons are going quite well. I am playing a lovely soft piece, but I can't remember the name of it. Must go and post this letter now.

Yours lovingly, kissingly and affectionately forever,

Jonathan

Johnny with Indian Headdress

Love heart from Coleraine

Johnny with Top Hat

Johnny kissing mum on the cheek "Food and Love"

Dear Mum and Co.,

I've recovered from my cold. The weekend at David Evans's house was good fun. On Saturday afternoon we went blackberry picking. We then made jam. It was delicious. Afterwards we watched a funny video. On Sunday morning we climbed trees, played on the bikes and cycled to an old quarry which is now a field of blackberries. In the afternoon we picked loads of rhubarb and made delicious rhubarb and cinnamon jam. When I got back to school I wrote to Grandma and Toby.

xxxxx, J

---

29 November 1989

Dear Mummy and Family,

Hope you are all well. I have a bit of a cold and have 'staved' my finger playing rugby in the A's and B's practice match.

Under XIV Rugby team at Coleraine

I have been doing exams, which have been quite easy so far—even Greek. The most difficult was technology. I have been revising in the library every afternoon. The rehearsals for the carol service are over. It is on 17 December. I wish you could come, but I'm aware you must take Cheryl to Cambridge that weekend. I'll phone Grandma this afternoon, but don't have much more news. I am looking forward to coming home at Christmas, and hope that we are having people round on the 24th. The Christmas lights are on in town, and that makes me even more excited.

Lots of love,

From Jonathan

PS In art I am doing a composition about electricity. I am doing Christmas lights.

I love you forever, again!

Jonathan

PPS I've run out of money!!

Entanglement. Light project at Coleraine

Christmas project at Coleraine

Dear Mum and Co,

I have enjoyed my first weekend back and have settled in well . I have a nice weekend coming up as I'm going to stay at Robert's which will be good.

Charlie is leaving !! The 2nd years have been bullying him since September . One of the boards on my bed is broken because the boys were jumping on it when I was away. D. Brown has written an anonymous letter to Matron saying who broke it. I am learning to play the *Londonderry Air* and *Abide with me*.

All my love hugs and kisses 67 times.

Love ,

Johnny

PS when are you coming over

To Home,

  I am feeling rather terrible at the moment and had to have an antibiotic for my sinusitis. On Friday I went into town to see Lauren, then I went to David's on Saturday morning. We played on the farm all day, and then in the evening we watched *Octopussy* and *Malcolm*. Malcolm is a mentally handicapped boy who helped make two robbers rich. He is mechanically minded and likes inventions. He makes waste bins with remote control cars in them to raid a bank. On Sunday we played *Commandos*, made huts and booby traps in the forest and went on the three-wheeler motorbike. It was good fun being with a family and making delicious egg sandwiches for tea.

  I wasn't a bit well at the beginning of the week and spent Tuesday from 11 a.m. till 9 p.m. in sick bay. Matron says it is homesickness, and I think so too. Matron asked Lauren to come up to talk to me. She cheered me up. Must go.

  Yours affectionately,

  Jonathan

  xxxxxxxx

  PS Each 'X' means a MILLION!!!!!!

Postscript on a letter from Johnny while at Coleraine

To Mummy and Daddy,

I would like to tell you how much I hate it here. I can't sleep at night, am always sick and am left out in most games. I try to sound happy on the phone, when I am feeling worst of all. I try my hardest not to think of you, but the more I try the worse it gets, and I feel worse and worse…

My eyes have no more tears left in them, so I am full of depression. I try to look happy, but deep inside I am in the depths of despair. Each night I sit up thinking, hoping and wishing I could leave here. It is like a prison. I am extremely eager to leave here and get home as soon as possible.

Yours sincerely,

Jonathan

---

7 September 1990

To Dad,

I would like to tell you my feelings about being at this school. I like the actual lessons and sports during the day, but I absolutely hate the boarding department.

These are my reasons:

1. I miss home.
2. I have hardly any friends.
3. The food is absolutely disgusting, and I hate it.
4. I only get home four times a year, and there is nothing to do at the weekend.
5. I can never get to sleep.
6. I have nothing to do on the weekends.
7. There is nowhere to go to play games, read or watch TV on the weekends.
8. The older boys in the third-form always annoy me.
9. I miss home.
10. When I am here my life is a misery.
11. I hope that you appreciate my feelings.

Love from Jonathan

Coleraine Inst.

Castlerock Road,

Coleraine,

Northern Ireland

Dear Mum,

How are you? I'm fine. School has been okay, and I've quite enjoyed it so far. I got a letter from Cheryl and one from Nick Mulholland. He sent me some photos as well. In one of the photos, he was flying.

I have been working hard, so the week has gone very quickly. In geography we have been learning about crystals, which is interesting, even though I don't like the subject. In history we are learning about the World Wars, which is brilliant. Latin is quite good at the moment, and we are learning about Aquae Sulis. This is the town of Bath in Roman times. I have no time to waste these days, but it is good fun. I'll send you another letter soon.

I love you lots and lots,

From Joni xxxxx

PS See you soon.

PPS Tell Dad thank you for the holidays and for giving me the opportunities, and that I love him.

PPPS Love to Cherry too.

Bye-bye,

Joni xxx

CAI

Dear Mum, Dad, Cheryl and Nick,

I had a good time this weekend. On Friday I went to Scouts, passed my swimming badge and went downtown to meet Lauren.

In the evening, I went to see *Anne of Green Gables*. It was excruciatingly brilliant, and Lauren acted wonderfully. Lauren's teacher, Ruby, and an old matron bought Nick and me an ice-cream. On Sunday I went to church. It was a nice Remembrance Day Service.

All my love,

Joni

PS I have enclosed the picture from the paper and the programme for the play.

CAI

17 September 1991

Dear Mummy,

School seems to be a lot more enjoyable than it has been in previous years, probably because I now only do the subjects I am most interested in. Also, I have my own study, which makes it easier to concentrate without interruptions. As yet we are not allowed to put up any pictures on the walls, as they have painted them PINK, but we have all decorated our doors and windows. We are waiting for noticeboards to arrive.

I have been put in the position of first violin in the school orchestra. The piece I have to play is terribly difficult. The concert that Robert, Darryl and I are going to is on 11 October at the University. We will be staying at Darryl's house in Templepatrick. I think it will be excellent. You will need to write a letter asking permission for me to go out on Friday afternoon.

On Sunday we went to Portrush. I thought it was a bit boring, but at least Darryl and Robert got girlfriends. Robert wants me to come over for a couple of days before we start back at Christmas, as his parents are having a big do and Robert has to arrange a table of twelve people. It will probably be *très grand*.

We were told last week that the second deposit of £144 for the ski trip has to be in by the end of September and the final deposit by the end of October. You will see the plan de piste (track plan) I have enclosed; also ,a picture of me at J's house and a tape I have recorded for Lauren. I think she will love it, as it is the best tape in the world. Well I must go, as I have to finish reading *Animal Farm* and start *How Many Miles to Babylon?* by Jennifer Johnston.

All Lauren's friends say hello to her.

Lots of love to you and the family.

Hope you are all well.

xoxoxoxoxoxoxoxoxoxoxoxooooo

To Mum,

How are you? This week I did athletics. I had a go at the shot put, but I could not throw it. It weighed a ton. I also did the long jump. It went quite well. On Saturday afternoon I watched the Grand National at the leisure centre with two other boys. I backed West Tip to win, but he came second.

In piano I am learning 'The Happy Farmer'. The teacher is quite pleased with my progress. I bought the tape of the musical *Joseph* with my pocket money.

Love Joni

XX 1,000,000

OO 1,000,000

Dear Family,

I am looking forward to seeing you all at half-term. I have asked my friends about Jurys and they all say it is brilliant. James O was there about two weeks ago when he went to see the International rugby match.

I may go to Grandma's this weekend, as I'd like to go into Belfast with D on Saturday. I also have to get Lauren a birthday present. D's parents are divorced, so he spends some time at each of their houses over the weekend and can't have anyone to stay.

A boy in the school wants to buy the brown denim coat that I bought in Spain a few years ago. I don't know if I should sell it, even though he has offered me a good price (£30); but I need your permission first, and he understands that.

I got a new pair of school shoes. They are really nice Dr Martens; they have steel toecaps. They were the most reasonable of the range, as they were old stock. I hope Cheryl's exams went well and that gets the grades she needs.

I went to see *Home Alone* at the weekend. It was really funny. It is about a boy who lives with a big family, and he gets left home at Christmas when they go on holiday and forget to take him. He sets up lots of traps to stop thieves getting into his house.

I went to have a mould fitted on Monday for my gumshield, and I've started into the book I got for Christmas, *The Lord of the Rings: Part 1*. It is the sort of book I like to read. It is a far-out fantasy, and once I start reading I can't stop.

Looking forward to seeing you. It would have been nice to see Cheryl. It's a pity she can't come to Dublin. Must close now.

I love you loads and loads.

Joni

PS I was wondering if I'd be able to go on the ski trip this time next year. It will be my last opportunity, and everyone else in the year is going. BUT, I'm sure it will be a lot of money. I could start saving up, as I know money is scarce and my friends all have jobs to work at. Well, I'm sure we can talk about it another time.

PPS Could R come for a week or so in the summer?

I love you,

Joni

13 January 1992

Dearest Mummy,

How is everyone at home? I'm surviving. The Formal was great fun, and as you see we all looked quite smart in our outfits. We danced most of the time, and we were wrecked at the end of the evening. We got home at 1.30 a.m., having been picked up by Robert's mum and dad. We couldn't sleep, so we watched TV and ate chocolates. I hope you like the pics.

Did Emma Nelson phone Lauren? I gave her Lauren's present. She was very pleased. On Saturday I went into town, as there was nobody about up at school. In the afternoon, I was with Julie; she was doing the last of her shopping in the sales. On Saturday night one of the boys got pizza to share.

Church as usual on Sunday, as it is the only place you see anyone—that is if you are looking. I had a sociable hour while a priest from Armagh 'blethered on' about people being 'couch potatoes' (people who sit on a couch and eat potatoes their whole lives). It wasn't the slightest bit interesting.

In the afternoon I went ice-skating with Caroline and then had tea at her house. I've never eaten so much in my life. It was really good. I am looking forward to the dry skiing on Friday, and am really excited about doing the real thing. We are flying direct from Belfast to Lyon, and then the hotel is a three-hour drive. I can't wait! Thank you so much for making it possible. I've just eaten my last digestive biscuit. I thought I had half a packet left! Oh well! I got my money changed today, and looked around for the best rate of exchange. I found one at 9.99 francs to the pound—the best about. I was charged some money as an exchange fee, but it was only a pound or so. I do hope Kim is fit and well again and that his birthday wasn't too much of a disaster.

Has Dad had any golf competitions lately? I wish I could have gone to Lauren's play.

All my love to everyone. I might write again next year! Joking!

Love Joni xxxooo

PS Can you send a photo or two to Cheryl?

I love you. Bye-bye.

11 February 1992

Dear Mum, Dad, Lauren and Nick,

How are you all? Yesterday I had a temperature of 102 and stayed in bed all day. I'm still not feeling too well, but I forced myself to go to school this morning.

As I have a bit of time on my hands, I thought I'd write a letter to tell you a bit more about my trip. We left school at about 10.30 a.m. on Friday to get the 1.30 p.m. flight. We were really tired by the time we arrived at Les Deux Alpes at about 6 p.m., where dinner was waiting for us.

That night we walked around Le Village, which was the part of town we were staying in.

Next morning, we were astounded at the views all around. It was like a whole new world above the clouds, and we could see the church miles below.

Our skiing lesson started at 9.30 a.m. every morning. The first day was spent mostly on learning technique, and not really for fun skiing. I wasn't very confident at first, but after an hour or so practising I got to grips with it. In the evening R, J and I went out and had a pizza in one of the pizzerias in the main town.

The following morning, after about ten cups of hot chocolate, we went up the slopes. It felt a bit colder than the day before, but once you get moving you don't even notice the cold. By 11 a.m. the sun was shining so brightly that I had to take my coat off because of the heat. There wasn't any wind at all, and at lunchtime we lay in the snow with only our T-shirts on.

In the evening, we went ice skating on a frozen lake, which was amazing and well worth having the experience. We also went out to a 'Crêperie.' I had a crêpe with fresh cream, strawberries and peaches on it. It was absolutely delicious.

The next day we had our lesson as usual, except we went further up the mountain to some more challenging slopes. In the evening, we went to a place in Le Village where they did karaoke (however you spell it). It was a really good atmosphere. I enjoyed it and sang 'New York, New York' and 'Should I Stay or Should I Go'.

On Tuesday we went to the glacier and skied all the way down from 3,800 feet to 2,300 feet. It was brilliant, and the view from the glacier was panoramic. We could see for miles and miles around, and could even see Mont Blanc.

On Wednesday we went for a trip to another resort called Alpes D'Huez. It was a good day's skiing—worth doing, but the snow was a bit icy. The resort is well known for being windy, and I was blown off the drag a few times, but I was fine.

That night we went sledging on the lower slopes. Nick would have loved it. Afterwards we went to the Crêperie, called Eddys and had our supper before returning to the hotel by 11 p.m.

The next day we went to the very top of the glacier. It was fantastic, but very cold—fifteen degrees. In the afternoon, we were videoed skiing and then given our awards. Our whole group got the bronze. We nearly reached silver, but were not quite there. The instructor said we were an excellent Beginners group.

In the evening, we had a last look around the town, as we had to leave at 6 a.m. (5 a.m. English time). The journey home was quick enough, and we arrived at school at 3 p.m. on Friday.

I had a fabulous time. I really enjoyed the experience and would go back again without hesitation. I know you would love it too, even though you have all your excuses. I saw a woman who must have been seventy-five years old skiing, and there were plenty of boys with rugby injuries on the slopes too.

I was happy to go Grandma's at the weekend, and I had smoked salmon until it was coming out of my ears. I have never seen so much smoked salmon in my entire life, and I probably never will again. It must have been three inches thick.

All my work is up to date, so I went to the cinema to see Our Girl. I think you'd enjoy it. I hope all your colds have gone and that you are feeling much better. I really must close now.

Love you and miss you all lots and lots.

All my love,

Joni xxxooo

To Mum and Dad,

After the freedom of the skiing trip I have been feeling very unsettled. I have been thinking this over for a long time and have definitely made my final decision. I desperately want to leave this school. I know you sent me here for the best, and I appreciate that. Maybe I could go to Lewis Priory and get the train there every morning. There would be no hassle and I would be wide awake, as that is what I am used to here. If I was at home, I'd be under less stress than I am here. I don't think I would miss anything at all. If I go to a school in England, I will get better at music and get better nourishment. I promise you there will be no problem about doing homework. I'm used to doing this here also. When I am here, I am never at ease and get no chance to relax at all. I really want to leave. I would be so much happier, and it would be a lot less expense for Dad and you.

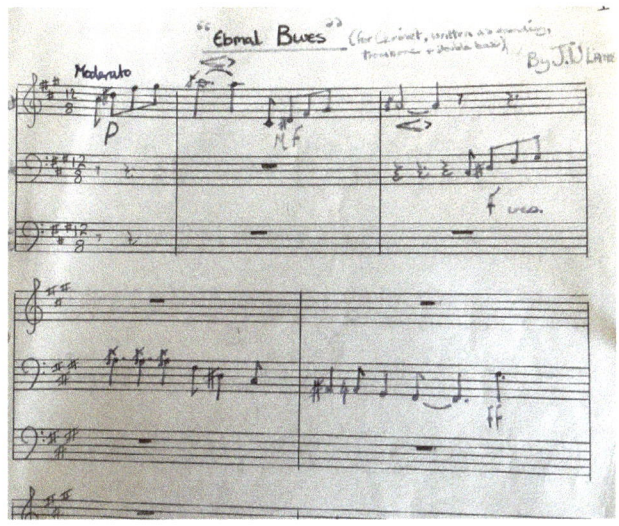

'Ebmal blues for clarinet' by Johnny Lambe

I have been thinking about this since the beginning of term; it is not just a spur-of-the-moment thing. I didn't want to tell you until I had thought everything through. I have now thought about the advantages and disadvantages, and have decided it would be best for me to be at home. I have no doubts about it.

This week I started a petition; out of 130 people, 120 don't like the food—including me. We are taking it to the head boarding master.

This weekend I am the only person in the year not out on a pass; it will be so boring.

I don't want a whole big fuss made. All I want is for you to agree to what I want. Please, please, let me. I don't want anyone getting upset about it. I just want to leave at the end of the year.

This week is so boring. I have no news.

Love from Joni

***

While I was in Coleraine I felt supported by the many letters from family. It was especially good to get some from Dad. This letter reminded me of how much we enjoyed The Waltons and how we would shout out "Goodnight, Mum, Dad, Cheryl, Lauren, Nick" before we went to sleep.

---

21 May 1991

Hi Jonboy,

Hope this little note finds you well. Things here are not great at the moment. The weather is poor, I am poor, business is poor; but still, it could be worse (I think). Mum and I are off tomorrow night on our second honeymoon (all lovey-dovey and hanky-panky). We are both looking forward to a break and hopefully a bit of sunshine. We sail from Newhaven at 10.30 p.m. on Wednesday night. When we get off the boat at 4 a.m. French time, we will drive to the Rhone Valley. I hope to make it to a town called Orange, where we will stay for the first night. Then we go on to Antibes, which is between Cannes and Nice, and not too far from the Italian border. Hopefully, it will be a good trip. We will send you a card and bring back some Carambars (toffees) and Hollywood for you lot.

It is the end of May, and we have just received a letter from Mr Forsythe saying that there is no problem with you stopping a week early. Mum and I will come over on 22 June (not long, eh!).

As I say, not a lot is happening. Not getting any supply teaching (I think I will have to vote Labour in the next election). Bring back Maggie. I got Mum a bike, so when we go to France we will all have wheels. I hope you are saving up for your holiday! Did you see St Lunaire Beach on the two episodes of *The Darling Buds of May*?

Well, son, lots of love, and good luck for the exams.

See you soon,

Dad xxx

2 February 1992

Magdalene College, Cambridge

Dear Jonathan,

How are you? I do hope you are well and not too homesick. I miss home a lot, but at the moment I am burying myself in work. In fact, I just discovered today that I passed the first part of my medical exams.

By the way, what do you think of the recycled paper? I am trying to do my bit for the environment.

How are the violin lessons going? Is your teacher still as revolting as usual? I've been playing the trombone a lot here. I'm in a band, and we have a party to play at tomorrow. It's really quite good fun.

Today we cut up 'Flossy's belly '(cadaver). YUK! I would like to send you her belly button, but I can't because we have to bury her at the end of the year.

Well, that's about it. It is really quite boring here. If you've got nothing better to do, then drop me a line.

Take care.

Love Kim

PS I'll see you in Brighton. Bye-bye.

---

22 February 1992

Jonni,

Hello. How are you? I promised to write. The main thing I want to tell you is that I've moved house since we last met (twice). I moved from Harrington Villas to a temporary, until we moved here yesterday. You can see the address above. It is near Withdean Park. I doubt if you know where that is! How's Ireland anyway? Enjoying yourself? How's school? I don't think I'm going to get a reply to these questions, am I? It is a very slim chance that you are going to write back.

As you can tell, I never write letters; in fact, the last one was the one I wrote to you.

Try to write back!

Till next time.

Toby

19 September 1992

Jonni,

How are you, you little git? Where's the letter you promised me. I guess I'll have to let you off, but if it happens again, I'll come over to Ireland and beat a letter out of you!

I suppose you want to hear the gossip. No thanks to you, half the population of Brighton is going around saying, "Molly, you in trouble girl?" If not that, they are asking the local shopkeepers if they value their windows and telling them they've got connections. Apart from this, Brighton is still a tad boring. I've got a local pub now that serves me without ID. It's The Old Ship opposite the King Alfred. Unfortunately, they don't sell Murphy's but they do Newquay Brown. Here's something that might interest you. Katie C. wanted to go out with you during the holidays, but when you asked her out she was pissed and can't remember saying no. Personally, I think Katy T. didn't ask her for you.

I've seen Nads a few times downtown. She says hello.

Write back soon or else!

Toby

PS Yesterday in school someone asked your dad if he noticed the stain on your carpet. You're safe.

Dear Jonathan,

I've heard that you are a wee bit homesick, so thought I'd write you a letter to cheer you up. At the minute, I am in the middle of my exams, which is a real pain. Chemistry was okay, art all day yesterday and maths this morning. Dreadful, but who cares? Tonight I am off out with all my friends, as Kim is going back to Cambridge tomorrow morning.

Things have been really strange since I went back to school. Phoebe is worse than ever; she and her little crowd of friends have dyed their hair and are wearing black leather jackets and Doc Martens boots. Do you remember Adela? She used to have lovely black hair; now it is dyed pink. Ugh, ugh.

At the minute, I am watching *Neighbours*. Dad and Mum are just back from a drive in a new car: a silver Magda with an electronic roof.

I expect you are bored reading this now. Just a quick note. Must go.

Loads of love, and see you soon. Huge kisses.

Your adoring little-big sister.

Cheryl xxx

Dear Joni,

At the moment I am watching *Octopussy*, so I thought I'd have a letter-writing session. All the exams are over now, thank God. I'm really shattered after sitting up cramming till after midnight and then getting up at 5 a.m. I seem to have slept all afternoon. We watched the Ireland match. Ireland lost 21–0. Poor Dad! I doubt Mike and Sammy will be doing a lot of celebrating.

I had a letter from Kim this morning, and he was surprised and pleased to have heard from you. So you should be getting lots of mail through the post, what with Mummy, Toby, me and now Kim. It must be nice. I hardly ever get any (think, hint).

I think Kim is enjoying this term, but Cambridge is meant to be freezing, so I think I might send him a hot-water bottle through the post.

Donna, Adam and Anna are here. Anna looks really gorgeous. She has grown up a lot over Christmas and is wearing really smart clothes. She's thinking of getting her hair permed. Donna isn't too keen, but I think it might be quite nice. Adam has a huge Bogun (Duork, I think). It's really disgusting, and its eyes move from side to side. I hope you are feeling better. I'm sure things will work out okay.

Love you lots, and see you soon,

Cheryl x

Hi Joni,

Not a lot happening over here, except today it is a bit like the hurricane. I have enclosed a few photos of my trip to Twickers which was really superb, despite the result. Someday I'll go over to Ireland and take you and Nick to a Rugby International in Dublin.

I hope you are remembering to be positive. THINK ONLY OF GOOD THINGS. When you receive this, it should only be fourteen days until Mum is over, two months until Easter and six weeks until your birthday. Any ideas yet? I bought you a nice pair of grey cords yesterday.

Well, son, lots of love, and remember your favourite song from *Annie*: 'The Sun Will Come Out Tomorrow'!!

Love Dad

***

I loved getting Grandma's letters, which were usually on a random scrap of paper and they always had a few quid inside. Gratefully received; thank you, Grandma xx

---

Hi Kid,

Hope this note finds you well, behaving yourself and doing plenty of reading and study. I hope you were listening to Mr Wylie, the trainer of the All Blacks: "If you can jump twelve feet, you can jump fourteen feet." I think that applies across the board. Take care. God bless.

Gram and Grampa

Hi Babe,

Hope this note finds you well and doing a lot of work. It will soon be Christmas, and I'm sure you are looking forward to that. Your grandfather and I are very tired, as we did a fair ten days ago. Anyway, we'll get over it. Take care. God bless.

Gram and Gramps

Hi Babe,

Hope this note finds you well, in good form, interested and doing good work, behaving yourself and looking forward to Easter. I will write again soon. Be good. Take care.

All our love.

Gram and Grampa

Dearest Johno,

I do hope you this note finds you well and doing good work. We will be away for two weeks, so enclosed! Be a good boy. Take care. God bless.

Gram and Grampa

Dearest Johno,

Thank you very much for your delightful letter and drawing. I do hope this note finds you well and working hard. All our love to you and Nick.

Gram and Grampa

***

I see Lauren quite often, as she is at the girls' school down the road. A letter from her was unexpected and cheered me up.

Dearest Joni,

How are you? I hope you had a good weekend and were not too bored. I spoke to Mummy on Sunday afternoon. She says everyone is well. It's Cheryl's birthday next weekend. I am going to get her present when I am up in Belfast. About next weekend; if you are going to meet us, you and Nicky better arrange what you are going to do. I'll phone you on Thursday for the details.

Sonya was very sad when you fell out with her. She's still madly in love with you, I think.

Do you know Paul Curry? Well, Sonya is in love with him too (poor boy).

At present I am watching the Women's World Cup Final! It is really funny. All the ladies are so tall and beefy. Do you think we should sign Sonya up for a place on the team?

I had my first tennis match on Tuesday. Cousin Jayne and I won the doubles, and I won my singles 6–2. It was good fun.

Mummy said to ask you how much money you have left in your account. I hope you are not wasting it. How much are you taking out at half-term? I'm taking out £10.

JOKE: What is a laugh? Sonya's reflection when she looks in the mirror. Ha ha ha. I think my jokes are brilliant! Don't you?

I can't wait to go home. I hope you are not too unhappy. I must sign off now. I love you lots, babe. My letters are almost as long as Gram and Gramps's, aren't they? Sorry!

Write back if possible. I'll speak to you on Thursday.

All my love.

Lauren xxxxxx

***

As you no doubt realise, I've been getting more and more frustrated at school. I was finally forced to write a letter of complaint.

Dear Sir,

I am going to get straight to the fecken point. I'm fecken disgusted with the teacher, Mr Martin (big red nose), history. He blatantly, irresponsibly punched me on the back, assuming I hadn't done my homework. This is his usual, fuck-headed, black attitude. Picking on me yet again after a series of previous earlier comments. In other words, HE PICKS ON ME! I want something done about him. He hit me hard on the back and followed this with a few lighter punches, all witnessed by the class. Whatever happens, I will make further enquiries to a higher authority. Perhaps he should be fired! Taken to court! Knocked the fuck off! Punched in the head! Have his bollocks ripped off! I hope these suggestions head you in the appropriate direction of punishment.

Yours,

J. W. LAMBE

Ball at Coleraine. Robert, Johnny and James

After the ball at Coleraine

***

Coleraine for me was fun weekends and good food with the generous families of my friends; but also, as I'm sure you have realised, it was boredom, frustration and homesickness.

Most memorable was my first ski trip. I will continue to enjoy skiing whenever I get the opportunity, and of course writing and receiving letters.

Skiing. Johnny Jason and Mark

Chapter 2

Brighton

1992

I was very happy to be back home in Brighton: walking into town to meet friends, picnics on the beach and Mum's food. I got a bus from my house to Brighton College, and often my friend Geraldine's mum (Judy) gave me a lift in her floral car.

If Coleraine was writing, Brighton College was painting. It dominated my life. I even applied and was offered a place at art school.

Brighton Seafront
Oil on Board

Self Portrait in Blue
Oil on Board

Street in Arles
Oil on Board

Roof Tops at Arles
Oil on Board

Still Life with Green Bottle
Oil on Board

However, I felt I would have difficulty funding all the art materials. In the end I opted to read History of Art at Manchester. Someone once said, "History of art to an artist is like ornithology to birds." I often regretted this decision, but I met and became friends with the greatest bunch of people I would ever know.

***

My birthday was always a three-day event: Paddy's Day on the 17 March, Geraldine's birthday on the 18th and—whoopee—mine on the 19th. This photo was taken at my eighteenth-birthday Sunday lunch with Irene, Peter, Aishleen and Sinead.

This photo brings to mind the words of Edna St Vincent Millay: 'My candle burns at both ends; It will not last the night; But ah, my foes, and oh, my friends—It gives a lovely light!'

18th Birthday Johnny Lighting Candles

***

Brighton College Grand Commemoration Ball was followed by the long-awaited interrailing trip with Jason and Mark.

Memento from the Brighton College Leavers Ball

Laura and Johnny at the Leavers' ball

A leaver!

Chapter 3

Interrailing

Day 1—Sunday, 9 July 1995

We got off to a bad start the morning after the night before at the leavers' ball. Mum insisted we eat a big cooked breakfast: "You need something in your stomach before you set off." NOT! We agreed reluctantly to keep her happy. Needless to say, we lost it on the boat. I looked back to wave goodbye to Mum as she watched us walking up the road to Mark's house. His mum had agreed to drive us to the ferry at Newhaven.

We reached Paris at midday, in blistering heat. Everyone felt worse for wear, hot and sticky. We left the luggage at St Nazaire, and after about two hours waiting at a bus stop we made it to the Champs-Elysées—the only place that anyone knew.

We cooled down in a fountain we found completely by mistake in the courtyard of one of the many arcades branching off the 'Champs'. The cooling effect of sticking our heads through the bizarre wall of water was just what we needed. Gathering our thoughts, and just 'being' for a short while, enabled us to continue up the Champs to the Arc de Triomphe before resigning ourselves to a Burger King—a not-very-economical meal to start the journey, but at least it resulted in a much-needed second boost of energy and enthusiasm for the remaining hours in Paris. We had just been away for a few hours. We were beginning to realise the amount of water we would need to survive in the heat. Following the meal, we returned to the wall of water for another soaking. We were admonished for being so slovenly in one of Paris's more exclusive arcades, so we decided to move on and find some new fountains to play in.

After struggling with the international operator on the telephone, I gave up the idea of phoning home, despite Mark and Jas getting through to their parents.

We then walked to Le Pont Alexandre III, realising all the way how dangerous the Parisian drivers are. We watched the boats on the Seine and spotted the Eiffel Tower. Unoriginally, we chose it for our next tourist excursion. After all, it did have fountains outside to play in.

I had forgotten how big the tower was from up close, and I found it almost surreal. We did not attempt to climb it again on our budget, as the steps might have proved a little tiresome on our first day after the leavers' ball. We were actually much more focused on finding the nearest fountain to bathe our feet in.

Bathing our feet became a water fight, thus soaking us all from head to toe. Then it was time to start making our way back to St Nazaire for our luggage, then to Gare du Nord for the train to Amsterdam.

We arrive at the *gare* (station) just in time to grab some water and beers before departing for the DAM [*Amsterdam* – ed.]. Too tired to talk, we settled down for the eight-hour journey, and hopefully some sleep, which proved difficult despite having had no sleep the night before and the effects of the alcohol. We reflected on what adventures we were going to have in the month ahead.

Day 2—Monday, 10 July 1995: The Dam

Grandma's wedding anniversary, in fact. She would have enjoyed playing in the fountains.

We woke up suddenly, after a brief sleep, to the sight of the ticket conductor. Being dazed and confused, we said, "Are you a policeman?"

Slowly, I begin to realise where we were: not yet in Amsterdam, but travelling through the flatlands of southern Holland. It seemed a lot cooler than it had been the day before; maybe because my shorts were still wet from the water fight. I changed into some dry clothes.

I found the countryside dull and the towns quite industrial, but as we got nearer to Amsterdam, a few windmills began to appear here and there along the canals. My foreboding changed to excitement.

The bustle of tourists, drug dealers, police and locals made our arrival at the station rather overwhelming, but after being given the name of a place to stay for the night, we went for a stroll into the city.

The first sight of Amsterdam itself was just as I had imagined it: canals lined with tall buildings, an array of brightly coloured barges and houseboats travelling on surprisingly murky water, and trams busily carrying tourists through the crowded streets.

Breakfast was first on our agenda. Shortly after, having been offered heroin and cocaine in the street, we sat down to a feast of bacon, eggs, toast, salad, coffee, orange juice and a variety of jams and cheeses. We were shocked at the openness of the drug scene. They might at least have waited till after breakfast!

Breakfast over, we struggled to put on our increasingly heavy rucksacks and then headed for the Number 32 bus to take us to Camping Vliegenbos, about five kilometres from the centre of Amsterdam, in a fairly rural, peaceful setting.

The campsite itself was like a colony of students from all over the world, all with their small tents and in groups of three or four. It seemed at first that squeezing our tent on the patchwork field would be a task, but fortunately, despite the hordes of students and now-punishing heat, we erected the tent in no time at all. We then collapsed for a couple of hours' sleep before our grand tour of the city.

Interrailing with Jason and Mark

Entirely by mistake we stumbled upon the 'Red Light District!' Canals and small streets lined with brothels, sex shops and smoking coffee shops, with the smell of marijuana wafting over us. We were approached from all angles by dodgy Moroccans trying to sell their wares. "EX-TA-CY?" was the question! On the opposite side of the road, large women were leaning from doors and windows baring all, and failing miserably to appear seductive, in any manner, with their offerings. "HELLO BOYS!" was the cry. Shocked, in fear of being kidnapped, pick-pocketed or completely corrupted, we hastened to a post office and supermarket.

We had experienced enough culture in one area of Amsterdam, so we retreated back to base, and the seemingly safe suburbia, each of us with conflicting thoughts about the liberal city, cup-a-soup, bread, cheese and ham. Abandoning games of Blackjack, we fell asleep for the first time to the sound of the stereo in the next tent.

Day 3—Tuesday, 11 July 1995: Amsterdam to Hengelo

Wakened up drenched in sweat at around 9 a.m., and sent Mark off to buy some breakfast from the camp shop: sausage rolls and some chocolate milk!

Would have liked to stay longer in Amsterdam, but the prospect of a good meal convinced us to go to Hengelo, where Jason's dad was to treat us.

We packed up the tent and then sat around the campsite listening to Pink Floyd until everyone was ready for the day ahead. Once again, we set off, lugging the rucksacks around in the heat.

On returning to Amsterdam, we left the luggage at the station and set out for the Van Gogh Museum (the cultural experience of our day). The museum is fantastic, and it is pretty overwhelming to see so many works by the great artist in one collection. Mark and Jason understandably didn't appreciate the visit to the same extent as me. Nevertheless, they only started to complain as we were in the closing stages of the exhibition.

Leaving the museum, we had an hour to spare before catching the train to Hengelo. I persuaded the others to have a last look at the 'Red Light District' and at least have a beer in one of the coffee shops to soak in a bit of atmosphere. The place we were finally daring enough to go into could not be described as particularly atmospheric. In the end, we were in too much of a rush to even enjoy a beer.

The train journey to Hengelo was pretty uncomfortable, as there were no seats and my nerves were bad, to Jason's displeasure! Soon we got talking to some mad Dutch people who helped pass the time on the three-hour journey.

Jason's dad and his business partner finally turned up at Hengelo, and leaving the rucksacks in the car, we set off for the first eating place we could find. We decided unanimously on the tourist menu: mushroom soup, delicious steak, chips and vegetables, followed by some sort of almond liqueur, which I refused to drink on top of the many pints of beer. We had a good and rowdy time, covering every conversation imaginable. It was time to head to Berlin on the overnight train.

Day 4—Wednesday, 12 July 1995: Berlin, Dessau, etc.

We awoke after what seemed like no sleep at all, rolled off the train and promptly fell asleep on the platform. Jason and I dreamt that we saw Steffi Graff.

I was aroused by the gruff voice of a German policeman who said something which I took to mean 'no sleeping on the platform'. So we were forced to move to another part of Berlin Zoo Station in search of a Corona or a Kronenburg 1664—anything to quench our thirst.

Mark had the clever idea of going to a place called Dessau for the morning, so that we could wake up and get dressed on the train. Too dazed to argue, we went along with his plan, only to find ourselves in the most unhappy town in Germany. Maybe we were on the wrong side of town. It seemed to consist of three shops—two of which were ice-cream parlours.

We hiked with the backpacks for what seemed like miles to a place where we hoped to swim in the lake. It was actually a small zoo with a few starved-looking animals in an area of non-English speakers. Luckily, Jason and Mark had GCSE German. We got directions to the lake, but we didn't bother going to it. We wanted to leave Dessau as quickly as possible. We made our way back to the empty shopping arcade and had a lunch of cheese, salami, ham and bread rolls, with coffee after. Mark and Jason insisted on having ice-cream sundaes, forgetting we were supposed to be on an economy drive.

This was, of course, an interrailing trip, and our next stop was Italy, some 1,400 miles away. It was a long journey, so we passed the time writing the following story:

THREE BAD BASTARDS

(no prizes for guessing who the characters were based on)

BOY 1

Once there were three boys travelling through France. Their names were Samuel, Eddy and Mike. They were only three feet tall, but they had magical powers. One day they decided to leave for the coast. Eddy, the leader of the gang, had to …

BOY 2

… decide on many things. He had been elected leader by silent agreement with the others. He put his ability to lead down to vast and varied life experiences. The others were happy to let him lead, as he enjoyed the power and would not do too many stupid things.

The three travellers boarded the train for the coast, very excited and anticipating the fun to be had by all. But this was not to be the case.

BOY 1

Mike had a bit of a lad-on-'E' head, and decided he couldn't go on without getting himself a score. To get the money, he went into a café, stood on a table with a sub-machine gun and a bazooka, and shouted at the top of his voice, "Any of you fucking pricks move and I'll shoot every mother fucking last one of you." (A hint of *Pulp Fiction*)

As this was happening, Sammy drove a tank through the shop window, got out of the tank and blasted the person on the till's head off with a hand grenade, shouting, "Cat shit, mother fucker." As you can imagine, this caused quite a stir …

BOY 2

However, this was nothing to the triumvirate of hard-core, ready-for-anything adventurers. They had been there, done that and got the T-shirt and the mug so long ago that it had faded in the dishwasher. They sat down to think hard about what they could do next.

The standard replies were: "Let's get pissed/canned/laid." However, things changed and it was out of their hands. It had already been decided …

BOY 1

They were going to kill Bill Clinton, the president of the USA, and this was their last opportunity. So they got on a plane to Washington DC. It was now midnight. Bill was in bed fast asleep with Hilary.

> BOY 2
>
> What happened next? There is still some confusion about the exact details. The tabloid headlines varied: 'Hilary Eaten by a Dog', 'Hilary Captured by Aliens'. Some papers will print anything to increase their sales!

BOY 1

Especially the tacky ones. I think it was a total mess-up, because rather than achieving their target (killing Bill), they became famous for catching Mr President in bed with someone who wasn't in fact Hilary, but Mystic Meg of National Lottery fame.

Sam and Ed were really pissed off, so they decide to go out on a killing spree with their new semi-automatic machine guns.

Off they went into the sunset.

They really were 'Bad Bastards'.

'Freedom' Johnny Jason and Mark

Hello Mum and Everyone,

As we are nearing the end of our interrailing adventure, I thought I should send you a few postcards.

Venice is absolutely beautiful—probably the most beautiful of anywhere we've been, along with Prague. At present there is a festival to commemorate 100 years of Venetian art, with over fifty exhibitions. There is also a Picasso and a Dali exhibition on.

Today we visited the Peggy Guggenheim Collection (of modern art), which was excellent. It is situated on the Grand Canal and is unique in that we could actually sit on the edge of the terrace and cool our feet in the water.

We have been staying on a campsite about half an hour from Venice with three Belfast girls who have kept me in constant hysterics!

Venice

Tomorrow we are off to Naples, and hope to visit Pompeii and see Vesuvius.

All my love,

Johnny

xxx

A Canal in Venice Pencil Sketch by Johnny

Hello Family,

We're in Rome now, having spent a few days visiting Naples, Pompeii and Vesuvius. We are staying halfway up Solfatara, a volcanic crater just outside Naples. We thought it was erupting again, as it emits jets of steam, but it was actually a big forest fire.

Rome is beautiful. Today we saw the Colosseum and tomorrow we are getting up early to visit St Peter's Basilica and the Vatican City. I don't think we are going to Athens. It is too hot to travel over 1,200 miles to get the ferry from Santorini to Athens. We're going to Florence next, and then the South of France and Barcelona.

Hope everything is well at home.

Lots of love,

Johnny

Hello again Everyone,

I'm still in Rome. We visited the Vatican City and the Sistine Chapel, which were really interesting. However, it was thirty-seven degrees at midday, and we had to wear long clothes. Therefore, it was a bit exhausting, but really worthwhile.

Here is a picture of John Paul II for the wall.

Love Johnny

Chapter 4

Manchester

1995

Dad drove to Manchester for the start of the first term. Chatting on the way there made the journey seem short. We asked a student for directions, found the halls of residence, unloaded the car and then it was time to say goodbye. Mum tried to hold back the tears, but was visibly sad. Her awareness of the 'empty nest syndrome' was heightened, as was the need to accept that I was going to be immersed in university life and would have little time for calls or letter-writing. Dad told me later that Mum cried all the way back to Brighton.

As always at the beginning of a new adventure, I was happy and excited. Mum proved to be right: I didn't get round to writing to her until the end of November.

> Hi from Manchester, Mum,
>
> Sorry it's taken so long to write to you, but with so much work to do, and my job, it keeps slipping my mind, and I forgot to post the letter.
>
> The charge on the American Express card actually did bounce in my account, for which I was charged £80. I realise now what happened. There was so much money going into and coming out of my account. The first chance I get, I will put it in your account along with the remaining money.
>
> I am working most nights as it is, and to work days would mean I could not get on with my university work, which I'm sure you'll agree would be slightly foolish at this point.
>
> I'm not sure about applying for the MA course, as I don't want to start until Autumn 1999. It will cost me £100, which I can't afford. Not that I'm moaning. There is enough money to eat from what I am earning; it's just that other things are not really viable right now.
>
> I am looking forward to getting home for Christmas, having a rest and spending time with the family.
>
> I must go now, as I have to finish typing up an essay for tomorrow.
>
> All my love and best thoughts,
>
> Jons xxx

***

The Art History tour to Paris was one of the highlights of the course. Arriving at the Musée Picasso, I felt immediately comfortable. The staircase and entrance hall were flooded with bright sunlight, and such a dramatic entrance was surely a promise of an inspiring and fulfilling exhibition. The museum is immaculately arranged with an abundance of large airy spaces, making it very user friendly. The advantage of a single-artist museum was apparent to me, especially when the artist was Pablo Picasso.

Picasso is called 'The Catalan Artist'. Picasso was not a Catalan, as he was born in Malaga, but he lived in Barcelona for several years after his father took a position at the School of Fine Art. The Picasso museum in Barcelona, and the Parisian Gallery, to me are incomparable. Barcelona concentrated on Picasso 'The Catalan Artist' and the status symbol. This exhibition is a journey through the artist's life. The Parisian Gallery is a homage to Picasso's brilliance. It represents the internationally renowned artist. The problem for me was choosing pieces to focus on, as I was excited by them all. I viewed the exhibition twice before I could make my choice.

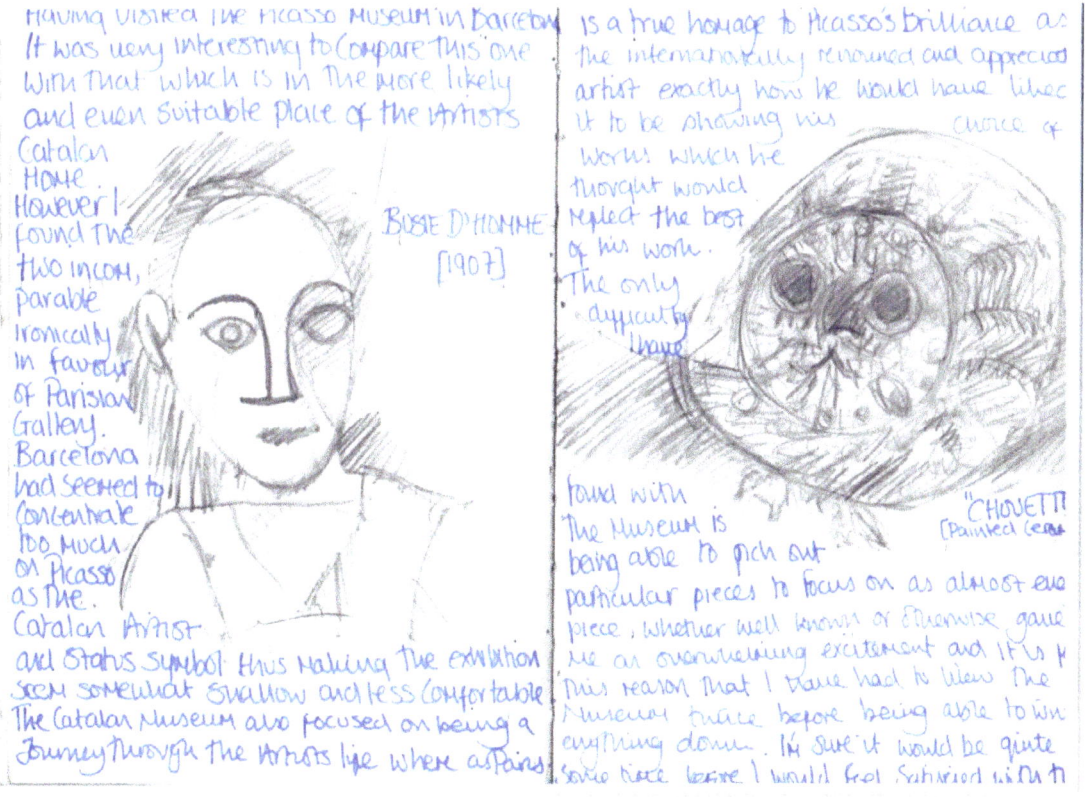

Le Musee PICASSO BUSTE D'HOMME 1907 and Chouette Painted Ceramic

I was struck by the power of his sketches and drawings in the temporary exhibition, by his academic paintings and by the range of styles, right through to his latest works.

The first painting to capture my attention was *L'Acrobate*.

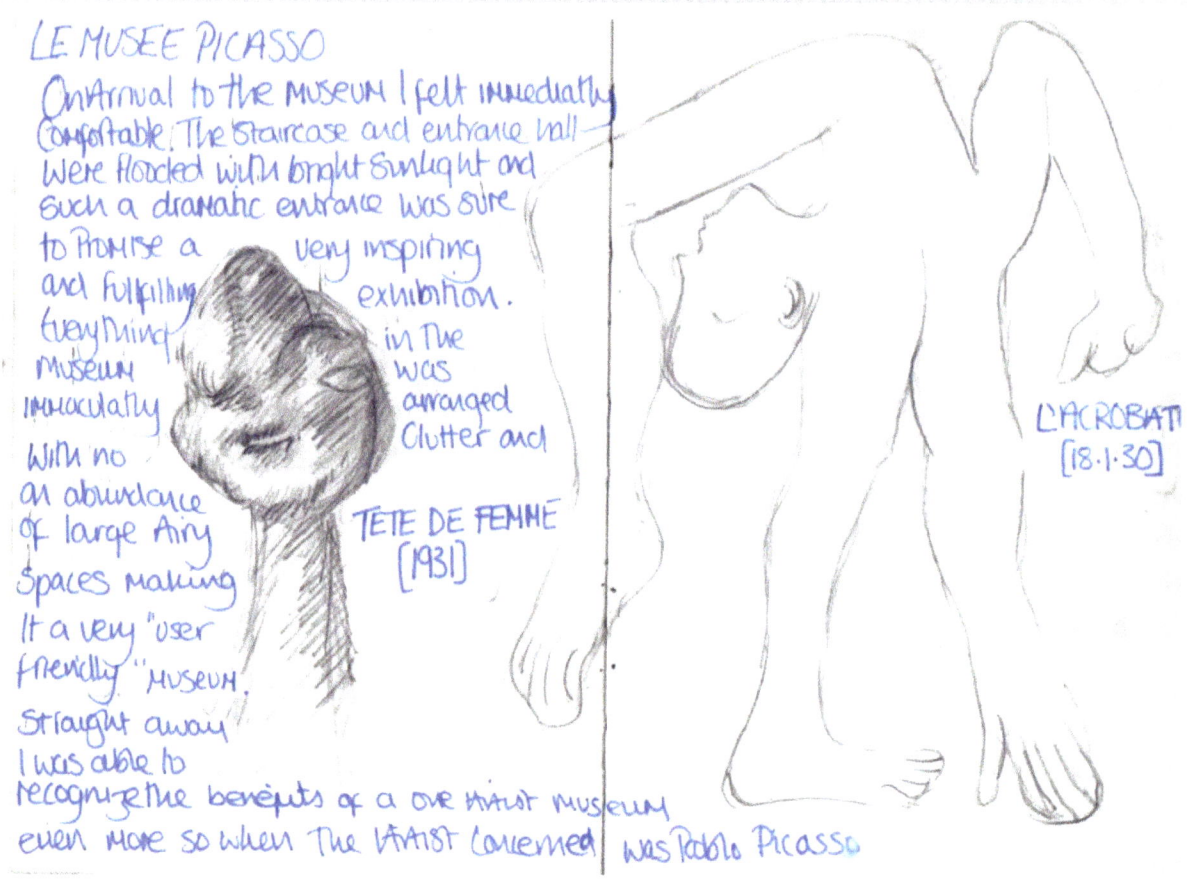

Picasso Tete de Femme 1931 and L'Acrobate 18.1.30

It is one of his simpler works, painted in one day, using a black outline and two shades of grey to highlight a basically solid shape. It is simplicity and perfection, an example of what can be achieved at speed.

Picasso wanted people to be moved by his art. The emotion in Picasso's figure paintings is powerful. Many of the figures are exaggerated and even distorted. In *Les Deux Femmes* we see two women running with abandon along the shore, hair flowing behind. The brilliant blue of the background highlights the earth tones of the rocks and the flimsy 'dresses' which cling to the body. Heavy rustic limbs and arms reach out for freedom, with the emphasis on the female form—one small breast peeping out and a large breast swinging as they run. Here we see passion unleashed—a dash for freedom. The muscular bodies and the strong feeling of motion are perhaps representing the cult of sport and fitness of the post-war era. There is no return to pre-war order or the classical past. Perhaps in this we see the shock of the new.

Deux Femmes Courant sur la Plage 1922 Gouache

The powerful sense of motion in *Les Deux Femmes* (1922) can be contrasted with the stillness we see in *L'Etreinte* (The Embrace) (1903). Are the nude figures at one with the environment or is there a sense of even embarrassment to be exposed? The heads are bowed and hidden from the artist's gaze. The female almost appears to be comforting the man. Her arms around his shoulders, he holds his head in his hands. This work asks questions of us. Is this a gentle painting of calm, of serenity, of fulfilment, or is it a picture about loss? Here is a room with a bed, and drapes drawn back, so no barriers. Is it a representation of before or after a scene? Is this a pregnant stomach or is it a 'baby tummy' pressing on his limp member? Is the apparent stillness and serenity of this representation real, or in their tender embrace are the young couple comforting and supporting each other after a loss? Our emotions are aroused and we are moved to ask questions.

Picasso

I was far more able to relate to the emotion in Picasso's figure paintings than many of the older works which I had seen in the Louvre. Although many of his figures are larger than life it is their gentleness which is immediately striking. His nudes seem uncomfortable and even embarrassed at their exposure. This naivety is somewhat contradictory when their size is taken into account but Picasso is able to let only their sensitive qualities shine through. "Grand nu à la draperie" [1923] and "Grande baigneuse" [1921] show the figures naivity and embarrassment by the presence of drapes which the figures use to hide their exposed bodies. It is also seen as they have underdeveloped breasts in comparisson to their oversized limbs.

The cubist element is clearly visable in these two paintings as Picasso has made up his figures using only a small assortment of three dimensional shapes — the cylendar, the pyramid and the sphere. The brightness of the light shining on these figures adds emphsis to their exposure. "L'etreinte" [1903] - Blue Period shows a real feeling of love + compassion between the embracing couple. They, unlike the two figures I have just discussed, have no embarassment of their nudity and show great comfort in each +

L'ETREINTE [1903]

Picasso Etreinte 1903 Blue Period

In contrast to *Les Deux Femmes*, *L'Etreinte* reveals a theme running through Picasso's work. Produced in Barcelona just after WWI, this large pastel painted in blue and pink is a tender scene with hints of the melancholy of Picasso's 'blue' period. It is a depiction of a nude man and woman embracing in a bedroom. Initially, the image evokes a gentle feeling of peace, love and compassion, as she appears to be offering sympathy and support. It appears to me that the woman has lost her child, and ironically it is the man who is finding it more difficult to come to terms with this. She comforts the male figure, who holds his head in his hands. The faces are hidden from view, as the woman and her partner— this couple—are lost in each other, unaware of the artist's gaze. Picasso fulfils one of his artistic aims: to evoke emotion in his art and ask questions of us. The male figure, rather than the pregnancy or not, seems to me to be the main focus of the painting. We are overwhelmed by a sense of loss.

Walking through Jardins des Tuileries to the Musée de l'Orangerie, I had a flashback of a picnic we had with the Canadian cousins. It is a relief to be in the comparative calm of the museum with its Impressionist and post-Impressionist paintings.

I am immediately captivated by Chaïm Soutine (1893–1943). Especially appealing to me are his urban landscapes; the irregular shapes, the broad, sweeping brush strokes, and the dynamic use of colour, redolent of Munch (e.g. 'Paysage avec Personnage'), create movement and the bursts of energy by which we can enter the image and feel the power of a storm as seen in *Paysage* and *Red Ladder*. The dark undertones and harsh greens perhaps hint at the destruction of natural beauty and the havoc that is caused by urbanisation.

L'Orangerie. C.Soutine 1893–1943 L'Escalier Rouges à Cagnes (1923) (*The Red Steps in Cagnes*)

Like his landscapes, Soutine's figures are distorted. The ambiguous, caricature-like characters are almost comical. The unnamed figures emanate ambivalence. They are neither happy nor sad; they just accept the status quo. *Que sera, sera*!!

 LE PETIT PATISSIER [c.1922]

 PAYSAGE

Soutine's fascination with dead animals as seen in many of his still lifes such as "Boeff et tête de Veau" [1925] + "Nature Morte au Faisan" [1925] also carries on his sentiments of concern for the destruction of natural beauty for Mans selfish needs.

L'Orangerie. C. Soutine 'Le Petit Patissier' c1922 and 'Paysage' View of the Town

I had visited the Louvre several times with the family, mainly because Mum wanted to see the *Mona Lisa*. Uncle Roy sent her a postcard of Da Vinci's famous painting when he was in Paris as a young student. She treasures it to this day.

First thing on Sunday morning, the Louvre was overwhelming, and it took me some time to find my bearings. The fourteenth-century Islamic art was an eye-opener for me. I was energised by the predominantly rustic reds, royal blues, aquamarines, greens and turquoises of the ceramics and textiles. I have no knowledge of Islamic art. What has survived of my GCSE French was a handicap rather than an aid to understanding. I feel that some information in English about the meaning behind the recurrent themes of the vine, animals, fishing and nature would have been useful.

Le Louvre – Paris

The Louvre

Aight like being thrown in at the deep end it's all abt overwhelming first thing on a sunday morning. It is such a vast museum with so many rooms and collections that it's taken a long time before I have been able to find my bearings and write something

XVIth Century Islamic Art

I haven't really looked at Islamic Art before but the stunning colours and patterns of the ceramics and textiles have really attracted my attention.

The colours which have been used are predominantly rusty reds, royal blue, aqua marine green and turquoise.

One particularly striking wall panel is "Panneau de Revetement à la bordure de pampres" which is mainly blue in colour comprising of two outer borders

Le Louvre

LE MUSÉE RODIN

This sculpture was commissioned by the Society of the Men of Letters. Rodin was known to never be able to finish his sculpture by the date it was required resulting in them ordering a court order against him. When this statue was finally finished it seemed to please the commissioners and they refused to pay Rodin for his work. Rodin said later that during his life, no other sculpture had caused him so much embarrassment as the manuscript that Balzac was paying out the "embarrassment of what he did

BALZAC (1891-98)
[oxidized Bronze]

- Balzac Strode in a highly intellectual and puts in thought. He is a figure of much prestige. It's probably quite fortunate that it is a dull day as the darkness seem to make the sculpture more imposing
- At first it seemed quite overpowering, alien but having sat with it for a while, I like and appreciate it far more
- The real power lies in its intense stare which has been created by the protruding eyebrows and deep set eyes.
- I think the eyes are the most expressive or important part of the sculpture as they link very well with the long, flowing robe which has no definite sense of direction in it.
- Rodin's sculptures seem to be pushing away from the classical style to a new type of Realism and Naturalism.
- In most sculptures he has focused on creating a multiple viewpoint

Le Musee Rodin 'Balzac' 1891–98 oxidized bronze by Rodin

This sculpture in the Musée Rodin was commissioned by The Society of the Men of Letters. Rodin was, however, unable to finish the sculpture for the date required, resulting in a court order being taken out against him. When the statue was finally finished, it failed to please the commissioners, and they refused to pay Rodin for his work. Rodin later said that no other sculpture had caused him so much emotional strain, and he felt that Balzac was perfect, and the embodiment of his style. Balzac stands in a highly intellectual—even arrogant—pose befitting a figure of prestige. The dullness of the day enhanced this somewhat overpowering sculpture. Viewing Balzac for a while, I realised that the real power is created by the intense stare, protruding eyebrows and deep-set eyes. Rodin is moving boundaries away from the classical style to a new Realism and Naturalism.

At the back of the garden there is the central circular pond. Four figures surround the pond as if performing a ritual dance. Oxidation happens with age, but the statues can be given a protective coating. It begs the question: why is one of the statues not oxidised?

The figure in the centre is one of the figures from *The Gates of Hell* (1880–1917). This was created before the other smaller sculptures, and it shows various scenes about the trials and torments of hell. It is supposedly about a man who eats children. One of the smaller sculptures reveals two lovers joined at their backs—united for eternity, but never able to see each other or embrace. This creates a sense of futility and gives a rather dissonant feel to the space.

Looking at the sculpture through the telescope adds another dimension. It not only allows you to view each section in detail, but it allows you to become a participant in the various scenes and evokes even more feelings of terror. *The Gates* are like a warning to us all, and its size and status casts a shadow over us. Rodin is perhaps inspired by Michelangelo and 'The Gates', a sculptural reference to the ceiling in the Sistine Chapel, and is suggesting that there mankind is more to be feared than admired.

Rodin did not always focus on the dark side of human nature. Some of his works are sculpted from white marble, this being the symbol of purity and a romantic element. *La Main de Dieu* intimates a gentle, loving God—the protector. The embracing Adam and Eve sleep peacefully as they await the renewal of life and love.

Rodin's most renowned work is *The Kiss* (1882). The lovers are entwined in a gentle embrace; the soft white marble reveals their natural beauty and innocence with no hint of sordid sexuality.

THE KISS [1886-89]

In the two sculptures "Le Main de Dieu" and perhaps more renowned "The Kiss" both have sculptures show the intimation of a man and a woman. But neither show to show the sordid sexual side but more that of love, nature and natural beauty. What really shows through is the purity and newness of love and life which is emphasised by the soft white marble of the lovers shown as opposed to the rough texture of the rest of the sculpture. The Hand of God is seen as gentle, protective and caring as it holds the embracing Adam and Eve as they step into existence the newness of life and love.

Le Musée d'Orsay

'The Kiss' 1882 by Rodin

My first impression of the Musée d'Orsay was the central chamber, with a symmetry created by its concentration on parallel, vertical and horizontal lines, redolent of railway lines. The lighting creates a sense of calm in the early morning, and there was none of the hustle and bustle of commuters. It may have had a different feel later in the day, with the arrival of the tourists. The clock on the wall was another reference to the museum's former life as a Paris railway station. Sculptures were empathetically exhibited, and it was good to wander in the quietness of the early morning. There is a compelling quality to these amazing sculptures, but I needed to view the rooms surrounding the central atrium. I felt these to be claustrophobic to the point that they made the paintings seem dull.

Vincent van Gogh (1853–1890)—My Favourite Artist

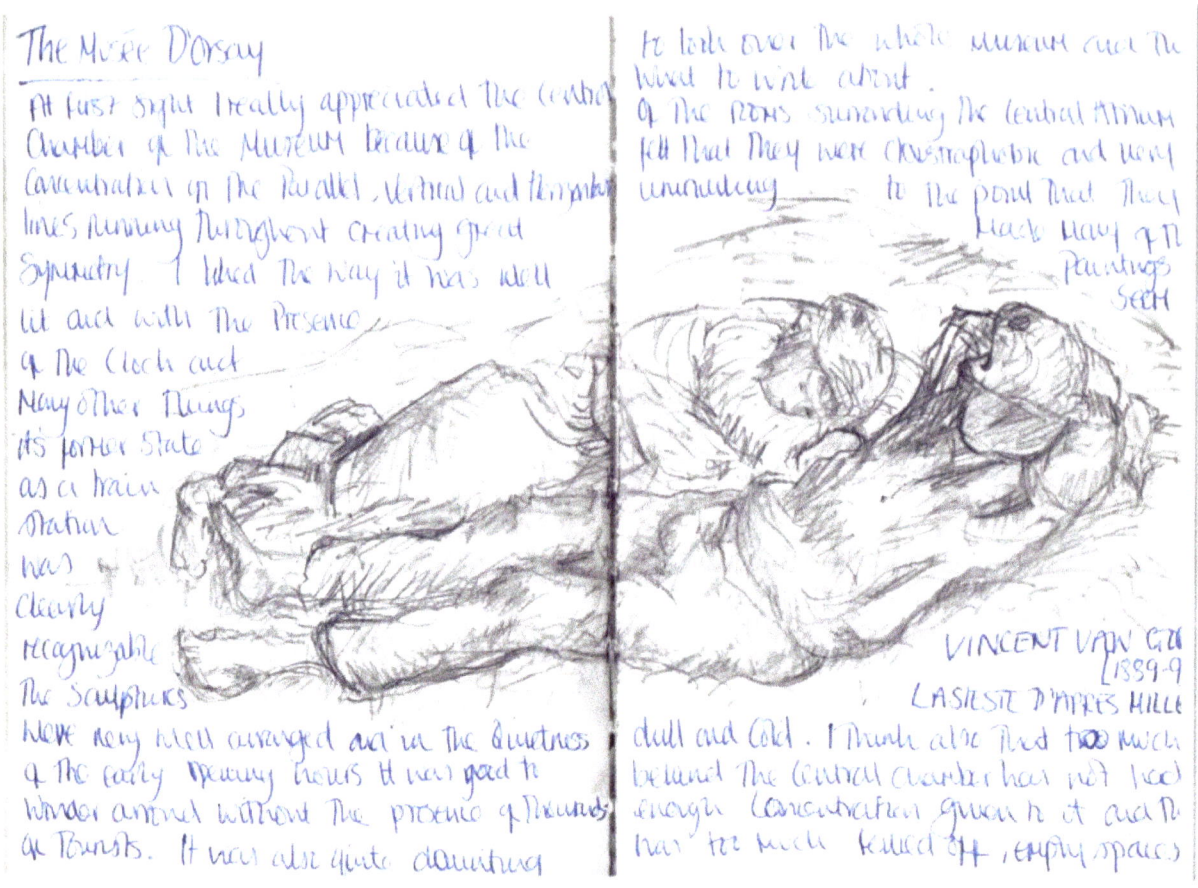

Le Musee D'Orsay. La Sieste d'Après Millet by Vincent van Gogh 1889–1890

This is the painting I would choose to have in my collection. I would have liked to see fewer fenced-off, empty spaces, so I lost my initial sense of calm, and it began to irritate me. My lasting impression contradicts my original impression, although the glass-tiled floors in the back staircase corridor created effective lighting. I am disappointed. It isn't authentic enough for me, and made me feel uncomfortable. I cannot find any link between the original train station and the Impressionists.

After the early morning calm of the gallery, it became for me an overcrowded, miserable space.

I do like the frame containing three works by master Impressionists. All of them the same size and painted in the same year. Each one typical of the artist's work.

Monet's paintings of Rouen Cathedral were on one wall in varying degrees of sunlight. Van Gogh was generally pleasing, but Gauguin and Seurat were confined to small spaces. The Seurat was especially badly displayed, as there was not enough space to stand back, thus defeating the purpose of Pointillism. In my opinion, the Musée d'Orsay should have retained its architectural integrity and never have been changed from its original purpose.

Having visited art galleries all week, coming to a cathedral was a refreshing experience; I only wish I'd had more time to spend here. At first sight of the Notre-Dame de Paris (as it was originally known), a medieval Catholic cathedral—in fact, the most famous of the Gothic cathedrals—we were overpowered by its architectural magnificence: the actual dimensions; the central spire; two towers, some sixty-eight metres high; three great rose windows, with the original stained-glass windows intact; the flying buttresses; and of course the magnificent doors with their early Gothic carving surmounted by the figures of Old Testament kings. The original purpose of this great cathedral, like many others, was to dominate the landscape and perhaps impose the power of God on the beholders. Our gaze travelled up these enormous heights to God, whose holy rays fill the church with splendour. It was truly uplifting. Does it achieve its original purpose? The answer to me is yes!

Notre-Dame has suffered much damage throughout the ages. It was desecrated in the French Revolution. Popular interest was aroused by Victor Hugo's novel, *Notre-Dame de Paris* (known to us as *The Hunchback of Notre-Dame*). Can we ever forget the sight of deformed hunchback, Quasimodo (Charles Laughton) swinging Esmerelda to the sanctuary and crying "The Bells, the Bells"? Since 1856 the four major bells on the northern towers of Notre-Dame have rung every fifteen minutes without fail. They rang for the liberation of Paris in 1944 and to honour the victims of 9/11.

Note: *Notre-Dame has been destroyed and restored often in its long history. Perhaps the greatest destruction took place on 15 April 2019. The world looked on in horror at the raging inferno. Mercifully, it was not total destruction, for the heavenly minded 'The Crown of Thorns' was saved, and for the earthly lovers of architecture, the three great rose windows and the two bell towers were saved. Work on the reconstruction of Notre-Dame commenced almost immediately. On the anniversary of the fire, 15 June 2020, the bells of Notre Dame de Paris rang out once again.*

I paid a quick visit to Sainte-Chapelle. This was the residence of the kings of France until the fourteenth century. Sainte-Chapelle is affiliated to the Catholic Church, but it has been secularised since the French Revolution. It is a home for Christian artefacts and is quite an exquisite church. The lower chapel has a sombre, mystical quality (perhaps a hint of the poverty in medieval France), enhanced by the lack of lighting. Upstairs (initially only accessible by the royal family) was like heaven: full of splendour and relics of the Christian faith. Perhaps this is the reason it was the first to be damaged during the Revolution of 1848.

La Grande Arche de la Défense is a spectacular structure, 110 metres high. It is part of the perspective of the Louvre and the Arc de Triomphe. Unlike the Arc de Triomphe, which is a tribute to the indomitable will of man evinced in many war victories, the Arc de la Défense to me has form but no character. This 'cube', with its cold concrete lines, felt morbid and bleak. This bleakness, perhaps heightened by the grey, wet day, was unlike the inspirational architecture of Notre-Dame and Saint-Chapelle, which lifted our eyes up to the beauty of the heavens. La Défense directed our gaze to the possibility of the more powerful France of the future: a strong France of wealth and prosperity. On one side you can look out to rich and prosperous Paris, but on the other the poverty of some of the suburbs is evident.

The choice of the inauguration in 1989 to mark the centennial of the Revolution was perhaps to appease the people—a reminder of the past—but also to heighten the awareness that France today is a secular society and the people are less impoverished. Today power is in the hands of the people, not with the Church.

La Defence

What a seismic year 1997 turned out to be. Most important to the family was Mum's fiftieth. We wanted her birthday to be special, as she has always made such a big effort for us. I wanted her present to be something she would treasure forever, so I decided to make a collage of a Venice canal for her.

Venice is one of my favourite places, and a place I would return to often. When the exams were finished there was a serious push to get it ready for the end of June.

The seed of my 'travel bug', I'm sure, was sowed when in Killarney, on a tour of Ireland, I cut my first tooth, aged four months. This seed was nourished by the interrailing trip around Europe in 1995 with Jason and Mark.

Summer 1997 I needed to escape the hard work and stress of student life, so I planned a trip with a friend, Alice, to Mexico; however, as the saying goes, 'Events, dear boy, events.'

There was a lump on my side. What should I do? I rang Mum. She said to make an appointment with a consultant dermatologist and she would travel up to Manchester to accompany me. He seemed to be a right miserable old git, and did not inspire confidence in either of us. Mum (decisive as always) got a private consultation for a second opinion with a renowned dermatologist in Brighton. In contrast to our previous experience, we met a doctor who was highly efficient, good humoured and able to relate to young people. There was no 'drama'. She said it was nothing to worry about, but to be sure, it would need to be excised and analysed. The excision duly happened, and good news—it was a lipoma. The dermatologist's advice to me was "Be careful in the sun." Mum was putting pressure on me to postpone the trip, especially as Alice had had a change of heart, so I would be going alone. My reaction: "I am definitely going. I will be careful in the sun. End of!"

50th Birthday Present for Mum
Collage Canal in Venice

Mum's fiftieth was a memorable day. The 'gang' were together for the first time in ages: Cheryl, Lauren, Nick, Stu and me. We brought the garden table into the breakfast room so that we'd have more surface space to prepare the food. We are all 'foodies', so that was a pleasure. We dispatched Mum (as she was nervous and excited and found it impossible to stand by and watch other people working) to the spa at the Grand Hotel for the afternoon. Great plan!

Mum returned relaxed and glowing after a massage and an afternoon of TLC.

The 'bubbly' was already open and we were in 'party mood'.

50th Birthday Party Mona (right) with Anne

At 6 p.m. an envelope appeared on the floor at the front door addressed to Mum. It was a letter from Mum's friend, Betty.

Darling!

I am so sorry we won't be able to come along to celebrate with you tonight. The clothes we intended to wear are on the bed ready for us to put on, but dear Mike's Parkinson's is not so good today, and as you know I wouldn't come without him. I was so looking forward to seeing you in the beautiful dress you described to me. Buy yourself a little treat with this. Sorry it's not more.

Mum was overwhelmed by Betty's kindness, so as soon as she was dressed she said, "Nick, can you drive me round to Betty? I will not enjoy the evening if I don't feel she can picture me in my dress and feel a part of the celebrations."

Nick, as always, was delighted to help. Betty was so happy. "How beautiful you look. I must have a photo of you with Mike. He loves a pretty girl."

We all partied till early morning. I had ordered an enormous chocolate cake from Chocky Wocky Doodah. It was very heavy, and I was ever so slightly worse for wear, but I insisted I should be the one to give it to Mum. The gang watched with bated breath. Oh dear! Another 'Johnny moment' coming up. I picked up the cake, but couldn't straighten up, as it was so heavy; crouching and weaving, the cake wobbling dangerously, I set off to deliver it to Mum. What with the low lighting, the weight of the cake and of course the bevvies, I headed straight for a lady, Sheila, who was not unlike Mum. At the last minute, I realised my mistake and did a magnificent U-turn, almost losing the cake in the process. Mum did not 'wear' the cake as everyone expected; it landed on her knee!! The gang and the guests erupted into whoops and cheers when the operation was successfully accomplished. One chocolate cake safely delivered to the birthday girl. As Nick said, "What an entrance!"

Mum's 50th birthday cake almost landed on her knee.

Chapter 5

Mexico

1997

BA ticket LGW to
Mexico City
14th August 1997

I set off on my Mexican trip. I felt nervous about the flight, but it ended up a complete party, much to the dismay of the stewardesses. I met the maddest person on the face of the earth—a Mexican artist named Art who passed out from drinking too much and some doting Mexican girls, and I was inundated with phone numbers, places to stay, etc. There was a good bloke called Adam who lives in Mexico City. I met two German guys, and we went together to find a place to stay. So, much of my apprehension disappeared. The beer also helped!

Arriving at the airport in Mexico City was a nightmare. The company (now about ten people) was worse for wear. We managed to get a taxi to the Hotel Isabel. This was fully booked, but thanks to some English girls, I found refuge in a place called Hotel Paris: a bizarre place, with balconies running around a corridor, glass floors and places to sit.

Easy Tiger.
Sketch Pen and Ink,
Hotel Paris Mexico City

The rooms left much to be desired, but we had a really nice little balcony looking out on a noisy street. Nothing left to do now but sleep.

A restless night followed. I finally awoke at 8 a.m. and went to find breakfast with Jan and Michael (actually Marco), the German guys. We set off to the Zócalo (central square), about five minutes from the hotel, and after much debate we chose a nice little restaurant where we had a huge but inexpensive breakfast: orange juice, bread, maple syrup, eggs, ham, salsa, tacos and coffee, which set us up nicely for the day.

Mexico City seemed really cool: people polishing shoes, Beetle taxi cabs, decorations and a huge flag at the Zócalo. After breakfast we headed for Piazza Garibaldi, the main nightlife music spot, but of course it was just after midday, so we sat outside and had a Corona and a coffee while watching the homeless sleeping motionlessly in the square. Lots of Mexicans in full costume were on their way to work and hard-core policemen with dogs, guns and bulletproof vests were patrolling the streets. We were now feeling tired because of the air pressure and jet lag, but we walked towards a market and stumbled upon a surprisingly prosperous building—the Museo del Palacio de Belles Artes—with lots of murals and an interesting exhibition of the work of the French artist Olivier Debré. Bloody amazing place!

Mexico City is fantastic, despite horrific traffic, the air quality and beggars (two years old upwards), each one trying to sell their wares. The vibrancy is almost palpable, as one would expect in the world's largest metropolis. Each zone seems to specialise in a different category of product, from the printers around the Zócalo, to bathroom furnishings, to fans, and even a full zone devoted to food mixers. We found a café, where we drank a Corona to the sound of Mexican guitar music, both live and from the jukebox. Mexicans just walk around asking if you want a tune played: "'*La Bamba*', señor?" Not I feel just for the tourists, but it is a part of everyday life.

By the market was a maze of shops selling everything from thimbles to hammocks. Ian and Michael (or 'Champ' as I decided he should be called) bought hammocks, hats and bags. I didn't purchase anything, but I'll be back tomorrow to get my hammock after I've been to Amex. My signature has altered so much since the last time I was away that I can't change my travellers' cheques. OH DEAR! A very kind businessman at the airport's Bureau de Change gave me 10 pesos to catch the metro. Decent bloke. Fortunately, I remembered I had some US dollars.

We were getting hungry again, and the boys didn't want Mexican (Philistines). I did understand; the menus are far too much of a hassle when you are tired. So we ended up back at the Zócalo at Shakey's Pizza Restaurant, an overpriced American effort. I ate a chicken baguette and *patatas* (potatoes), with a bit of MTV before retiring to the hotel.

15 August 1997

After the daily rain shower had ended, we headed to the Piazza Garibaldi to catch some Mexican nightlife. On the way, some Mexican girls asked if we'd like to go to a salsa night with them. We politely refused and headed on to our destination. The place was absolute madness. Everyone was selling something. Seriously. While we drank a Corona at the place we had visited earlier, we were offered infinite amounts of God knows what: yoyo, diplo, cigars, marijuana. There were lots and lots of singers, guitarists, drummers, maracas, violinists, accordionists, trumpeters, a one-man band, artists, shoe-cleaners, people canvassing for other bars, beggars, small children with dolls, and puppet shows, to mention but a few. Initially it was hilarious, but it became bloody annoying!

At about 1 a.m., after only one beer, we headed back to the hotel. I have never visited a more insane place than Mexico City, and I would be surprised if I ever do again. It is an unforgettable and wicked experience. We really have seen something of the Mexican way of life. Most surprising was how happy the Mexican people are. They must have to scrape pennies together in that manner their whole lives.

Mexico City is incredible; the noise and the amazing live music coming from every angle creates an extraordinary vibe.

Looking up to the moon it was hard to imagine that it was the same moon that we see sitting on the beach in Brighton or in the back garden of Albion Road.

Still yet to have a tequila! What a phenomenal day!

16 August 1997

Went to Taco Modo for breakfast: juice, coffee and tacos gringas—pretty good with lots of guacamole—which reminded me of the Mexican chilli dip we made for Mum's birthday.

After breakfast we make for the Zona Rosa to find the Tourist Information Office and an Amex. The Zona Rosa is an expensive area of Mexico City and appears to be completely detached from the old city. There are skyscrapers, banks, antique shops and top-name brand stores, such as Cartier and Gucci. There are lots of expensive bars and greenery, just like in any European city. The only reminder of the Third World were the children begging along the Paseo de la Reforma. A man was holding his daughter on his shoulders in the middle of the road in order to get cash from the passing traffic. She had balloons stuck down her trousers at the back to make it appear that she had a big bottom. Bizarre! Mexicans certainly don't seem too proud to exploit their children.

Anyway, Tourist Information wasn't too helpful. American Express was nearby, but I managed to change some money quite easily at another bureau de change. We found out bus times to Oaxaca and Puerto Escondido. We walked down the Paseo de la Reforma to Chapultepec, where we sat in the park and watched the tourists passing by while being the victims of Mexican kids who were determined to hit us with their football.

Chapultepec has many attractions: a modern art museum, the castle, the National Museum of Anthropology, a few small lakes and a zoo. Unfortunately, our late arrival meant that all were closed or about to close. We climbed up the castle walls, from where there are panoramic views over Mexico City, from the centre to the shanty towns on the edge of the surrounding mountains.

The first film in my camera ran out after two days, as everything is so incredible. Jan and Marco (Champ) informed me that I am a typically British person. I'm not sure if that is good or bad. They say I don't like to spend money and I have a dry wit, which in German eyes means British. I found this amusing, so I decided to continue travelling with them to Oaxaca. There is an Amex there, and apparently amazing views. This will compensate for missing out on San Juan Teotihuacán with its pyramids. I had decided against this, as Mexico City is so exhausting. Perhaps I'll return to Mexico City, as there is so much more I'd like to see. It's time to start touring Oaxaca which sounds great, and I've got companions, so why not, eh?

Since I have been speaking pidgin English practically every day since I left, writing in my diary is my only chance for a good chat. Surely in Oaxaca I'll find some Brits—not that I mind a bit, but it is extremely exhausting and I'm beginning to adopt a German accent. Can you tell?

Back to today! Having climbed the long trek up to the castle, we got on a bus then decided to get off at a random stop where we could find a place to have beer. We ended up in a cantina drinking Sol to the sound of the ever-present Mexican music. One of the waitresses was quite fun, and I spoke to a famous Mexican folk singer and bullfighter whose pictures were up all around the walls. We were treated like gods. There are not many tourists here, as everyone seems to be locals.

Jan decided we should get hold of some tequila *avec worm* or *gusano* to take back to the hotel. We found it without much effort in the form of three bottles of Oaxaca mezcal, with lovely juicy maggots in the bottom— mmmmm. We had a choice of maggot size, would you believe? Naturally, the fatter the better. Deciding to have something to eat first, we went back to the friendly waitress at Taco Moda, where we had been for breakfast. I had a Torta Milanesa (a dodgy pork type thing) with some fresh juice and a beer. Our 'friendly waitress' kept talking and trying to communicate with us. I cannot really remember her name, but we did find out. Naturally!

16 August 1997

My Spanish is getting pretty amazing. I'll probably be fluent by the end of the week— NOT! But I can say a few sentences or 'sentence-ettes' (phrases)!

We left the cantina and went back to the hotel, where we are now as famous in Taco Modo as in other places. We got locked out when we went in search of cups and limes. The cups came from Taco Modo and the limes from another random place, much to our amusement and that of the proprietors.

Marco made a phone call to Paolo, the girl from the plane, to ask her to come to Oaxaca with us. She couldn't, but she wants to meet us before we leave. I doubt very much that will happen. Returning to our hotel, we waited around for someone to translate so we could get back into Room 304. We decanted the mezcal into empty water bottles to catch the worm at the bottom. It went down a treat in our polystyrene cups with BA salt and scavenged limes. I didn't think it was having any effect, but now I know … I'm off to sleep.

17 August 1997

The thunderstorm from hell was going on outside. We sat in a shopping centre waiting for it to stop, drinking gin from the cups we got in the bar last night. The shopping centre is at the Coyoacán, an expensive and mostly residential area. No. No cantinas! Nor cheap bars! Ho-hum!

We went to check out the bus station for the evening's journey to Oaxaca. We checked in the bags and then went to the marketplace adjacent to the terminal, Orient, where we were herded into the first food hall and presented with a very traditional feast of burritos, rice salad and half a chicken. Since there were no other tourists in the market, we attracted a lot of attention whilst we ate our food with our fingers. The 'market drunk', who inevitably spoke no English, insisted on giving us more and more beer. There is NO ESCAPE!

"*Salut, salut, salut!*" is the chorus; the sole words of communication were in the form of a toast. He attempted to teach us the Mexican whistle: that is the one where you stick your fingers into your mouth and blow. I cannot do it. Alas, after an hour or so of sitting with this guy, the strain was beginning to set in. One-word communication was no longer amusing. Time to make a quick getaway.

We made our way to the Frida Kahlo Museum near Coyoacán. The sign for the 'Golden Arches' at Coyoacán proved irresistible. I had to test out the local Big Mac. There is nothing quite like a McDonald's to soak up the beer.

On visiting the Frida Kahlo, I discovered that it was forbidden to bring cameras into the museum, which was unfortunate.

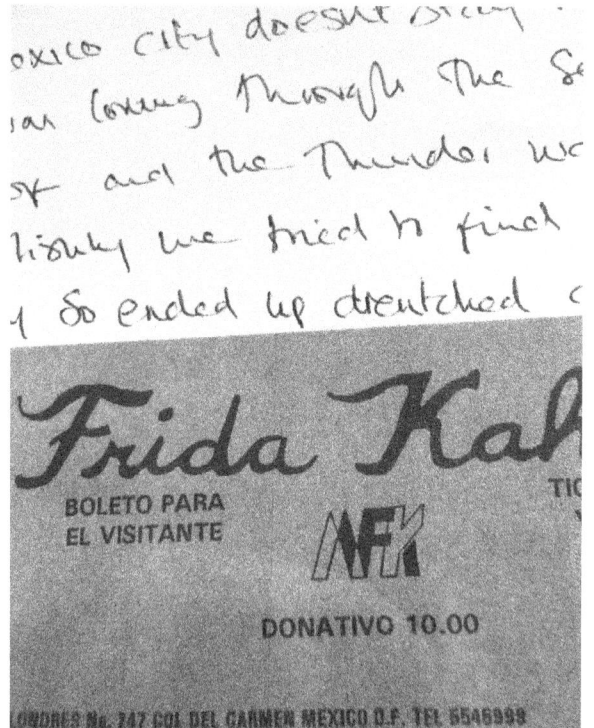

Visitor Ticket to Frida Kahlo Museum

The museum, the former home of Diego (Rivera) and Frida, was amazing; the villa, with its blue and white walls, was an ideal home, with cool courtyards and the best studio, still set up as it was when it was their home. The exhibitions were mostly paintings by Diego and Frida and their own private collection of works by Miró and Klee.

Also on display was their personal collection of Mexican arts and crafts. A copy of Kahlo's diary was on sale, but unfortunately at a very high price. It is an amazing collection of her thoughts and ideas in writing and paintings.

Around the corner from the Frida Kahlo is the Leon Trotsky House Museum, where he lived with his wife during his time in exile. We were too late to get in, but apparently it contains a great collection of his art, and you can still see the bullet holes in the walls and the furniture from an attempted assassination just before his death—COOL! The Trotsky is surrounded by a huge wall with lookout posts. What a pity!

It had just begun to rain when we went into the supermarket to get some food for the journey to Oaxaca. Ten minutes later an apocalyptic thunderstorm arrived. The rain in Mexico doesn't stay outside either. It came through the semi-permeable roof. The thunder was atomic. Foolishly, we tried to find a café nearby and ended up drenched and freezing in the shopping centre I mentioned when I started writing eight days ago. At last, after a cup of coffee at good ol' 'Maccy D's', the rain slowed down, so we legged it to the metro, having decided to spend our last four hours in Mexico at the bus terminal.

Bus Terminal. It did feel terminal! We waited and waited! The bus was late, but when it arrived we realised how much better it is to travel first class: TV, free Cokes, reclining seats, 'legroom-arama'—NICE!

I felt very contemplative as we left the city, watching the slums and shanty towns pass by while sitting in right wicked luxury. Exiting the city seemed to take forever: an hour and half to drive from the centre along a seemingly dark and endless tunnel. Eventually, I had that 'wow' feeling, when something completely new and exciting is occurring. This is what travelling is about. Now it was time to listen to some good tunes and watch the darkened landscape lit by the full moon rising high and far beyond my understanding. The smog had lifted and the air was ten times cleaner than the polluted atmosphere of Mexico City. I felt a mixture of anxiety, excitement and satisfied relief.

18 August 1997

Very early in the morning I listened to some good tunes after watching some Brooke Shields. Um! The landscape had changed from silhouetted suburbs to sheer cliffs and mountain ranges. In the moonlight it was incredible. These mountains and tunnels are straight out of *Lord of the Rings*; Good old Frodo would be right at home.

I dozed for what seemed like half an hour and woke up in the outskirts of Oaxaca City. It was 5 a.m. "Where the FUCK are we?" Got a coffee, met a French guy, got lost.

Finally, we got a bus to Central Oaxaca. Searched for a hotel; searched again and again. We settled on what is an excuse for a hotel and booked in! Posada Margarita, here we are! We were so tired that hell would have been tempting after our journey. We bought a beer. Shit! It was only 9.30 a.m. I woke up at about 2 p.m., then walked to the Zócalo along pedestrianised streets lined with low, rectangular buildings (nice architectural description, Jonboy). See *Lonely Planet* for assistance!

Oaxaca City is the state capital and the only sizable city. It is a Spanish-built city of narrow, straight streets, liberally sprinkled with lovely colonial buildings. There you go. Thank you, *Lonely Planet*; saved my brain cells.

This city has a very cosmopolitan feel and is much more relaxing than Mexico City. The grid-system streets are very user friendly. Amazing doors and Indian people selling their wares (in a less pushy way than those in the Piazza Garibaldi) have a movie-*esque* quality. The sun was hot, and the air crisp and dry. The sky went on forever and ever, with little fluffy clouds. I changed some money and went for a drink at the Zócalo.

It was awash with tourists. Oh! Something new to eat: grasshoppers! Not just yet; maybe later on. Balloon hawkers and boot cleaners lined the square, with the cathedral as a backdrop. There was a gentle buzz. I felt tired, yet more awake than I did in the gaseous streets of Mexico City. A British accent. BLISS.

We decided to head towards the Tourist Information Office, where we learnt the bus times to the ruins of Monte Albán.

Mt. Alban – White Mountain occupied by Zapotecs 800/400BC

The marketplace south of the Zócalo was buzzing. The Indian women and girls blew us kisses and offered their finest wares. I bought some 'I've been to Mexico' clothes. Oh, and I finally changed my bag. My purchases? A hammock at half Mexico City prices—150 pesos. Three man and good quality. Bargain! Cheered up by my consumerism—see, I'm not typically British—I was in the mood to eat something new. I thought I'd pass on the live worms, but "Give me some of them there grasshoppers". Not too good, but now I can say I have eaten grasshoppers in Oaxaca City. It's a good job Jiminy Cricket wasn't Mexican, or that one out of *James and the Giant Peach* (Mr Grasshopper). Rambla-arama! I've decided that 'arama' is a good word.

Aztec symbol for Infinity and Hardcore Techno Insect

On the way back to the city, we met the dodgy Mexican geezer. He followed us to the hotel … and then to the Zócalo. "We've got a bit of a clinger on the starboard bow!" Oh look. Lovely ladies. Oh, and you want to take our photograph. How nice!"

We got pissed with some people from Mexico City and were serenaded by a loud Mexican band. Alberto, the 'clinger', remained; I was suspicious of that one, but he got drunk and we found out that he is the local, friendly drunk, famous throughout Oaxaca. Still, this made no difference to me really. I did not trust the man whatsoever. The Mexican students all tried to be cool and British, much to my amusement. I sat back for a while and I realised what it feels like to be in the middle of nowhere: kinda cool and exciting.

When the bar shut, we headed to a place with live entertainment. We found a dingy bar where a band was rehearsing. The band consisted of: singer/main keyboard (Mexican Daddy), second keyboard (eight-year-old son) and drummer (eight-year-old son, who can play one rhythm to absolute perfection). CHILD EXPLOITATION? NEVER!

The kids seemed to hate their 'profession' and be old before their time. Their childhood is being stolen from them. In the drummer, there was a hint of the old man of the future. Funny in a way, but saddening! More beer, dancing, lots of students. Met some Indian people, a lot more relaxed than the Mexicans. We walked home through the streets of Oaxaca at about 2 a.m. Now I know the meaning of the word 'rowdy'.

This city is a haven in the desert. An eerie calm falls over it. It becomes silent and soundless. The electricity of the day is no longer present; it now has the dreaminess of a village.

19 August 1997

Excluding the arrival of Mexican Ginger, aforementioned, and despite the hangover and a case of the shits, today has been a relaxing day.

We drank Coke in a small cantina which only served three dishes: a plate of brown stuff, a piece of leather of some calibre or other and indescribable piss to drink!

"Let's go somewhere with a nice English menu, to nurse a hangover."

"Let's wait until tomorrow to go to Monte Alban."

We visited the arts and crafts market, with traditional weaving by Indian women who looked as if they had been doing it their whole lives.

We ordered a delicious European-style club sandwich and a glass of milk to soak up the alcohol. Sitting at the edge of the Zócalo, we listened to the music I'd selected for the pyramids: jazz. It worked strangely wonderfully with the atmosphere. I drifted off, feeling alone; but in aloneness, extremely content.

A siesta was in order, so we retreated to the hotel. Oh, yeah. More lovely ladies asking for photographs. We'll have to start charging soon!

Fell asleep pretty quickly. Finally , I get the true meaning of 'the shits'— no more daring food for Johnny. OW!

Jan and Marco had left the hotel, and I was awakened by none other than Alberto standing over me. WHAT THE FUCK? Why does this happen when

I am alone? Okay, it's safe enough. I think it's best to wait in the courtyard for the others to return. Alberto wanted money. I didn't want to give Alberto money, no matter how much he pleaded. Alberto could fuck off; but the problem was, he wouldn't. I gave him the money, praying that he would go away. It's for a taxi, I thought, but no. "Let's go drink, Terrazza." FUCK OFF! I just paid for you to go away, and you still won't. Get a life, please. What to do? I sat, trying to weary the bastard in the courtyard, drinking a Coke while he drank a Sol. Fuck off, please, I continue to think. Where are those BASTARDS?

By now I hated Alberto; I felt sick looking at him. He might not have had any harm in mind, but I felt trapped by his presence. I tried to look confident and happy, but I was obviously nervous and very pissed off. Okay. Right. I'll go and find the others. "Okay, I show you a good place," he said. Alberto had now infuriated me, but I felt empowered in the street. All I needed to do was walk to a busy place and lose him. I decided that the best place to look for the others was in the cathedral on the way to the Zócalo. Surely to God, he won't come in there. But, no; he followed. And I prayed silently as I walked past the altar. Any minute now I'll be able to escape. God, rid me of this terrible affliction!

Pencil Sketch The Dodgy Specimen

The Dodgy Specimen

I repeated it and repeated it in my mind. Alberto followed me into the Zócalo. Thank God, there was a crowd and a band playing. Thank you, God! Alberto introduced me to his cronies, who tried to sell me drugs. I wandered off, interestedly, into the crowd. At last I am free. Everything is great again ... and, oh look, here come Jan and Marco. I convinced them to turn around and walk back out of the Zócalo.

An attempt to find a better hotel failed, so we headed to the restaurant we had been to the night before. Had a burger. *Touristico* (touristic)! Hunger had set in and I needed English food. At the restaurant, two girls who had been sitting there the previous evening arrived and sat down at the table beside us. Coincidentally, they both lived in Brighton and went to the University of Manchester. Small world, eh?

Speaking English again was strange after six solid days of pidgin. I felt my vocabulary had really suffered. We decided to go back to the hotel for the rest of the evening. I felt happy in the company of my new-found friends, but as I drifted off to sleep, fear of Alberto returning to the hotel came back to me. Isn't it strange how something that appears to be relatively normal becomes the subject of a great story (ref: Alberto).

20 August 1997

The bus ride to Monte Albán was relatively easy, driving through the hills surrounding Oaxaca City on the dust track and in the blazing heat. I watched the scenery go by, and I felt great.

I'm now sitting here on the top of an Aztec pyramid, taking some time to write. The scenery is incredible. As I listened to 'Riders on the Storm', I had visions of the temples of the past with the brightly coloured Aztec people dancing and chanting in the central area of the site. It's quiet, as if time has stopped and the temples left to crumble. Lizards scuttle between the bricks.

Reality kicks in! I'm being bitten to death, even though I saturated myself with Autan this morning. Insects out here are a bit more hardcore than those in the city.

Monte Albán, or White Mountain, was occupied by Zapotecs from 800–400 BC and is now a tourist attraction with a coffee shop overlooking Oaxaca. Deserted, the ruins are now a place to contemplate and soothe the mind, as if the past watches over the future. Now I know why I am in Mexico!

20 August 1997

I seem to be getting more adorned with trinkets as the day passes. Maybe I'm going OD and will be found a gibbering wreck under a pile of friendship bands. It's time to bring out Insect Repellent 100. But, will it be strong enough? Who knows! What effect on the vocabulary and spelling? (exsistantuullsianism!)

Monte Albán does have an existential air.

Now for a little bit of Aztec art, just to keep the diary entertaining.

Back to Oaxaca to a cool cantina. We had just been force-fed octopus and chilli soup. I lost my appetite all of a sudden. Deary me; all I want is a nice sandwich. Is it too much to ask? The soup proved too much, so we had another beer and headed back to Quickly (or Q-One). Guess who was at Quickly: the English girls from Manchester and Brighton. For the fourth time, they were at Monte Albán too. Mind you, I think they should have gone to Blackpool on holiday, as all they do is whinge about the food and the Mexican people. But each to his own.

Hello again. I'm pissed. We went to the Zócalo and had our first Mexican tequila and a shot of mezcal—fucking harsh. It was like whisky mixed with turpentine, but I managed to contain myself and didn't throw up. Why does every Mexican want us to get drunk? We found a salsa bar—really cool. Mexican people have no inhibitions. They dance with much more abandon and pleasure than Europeans. Music is such a large part of their lives, and they are very poor, so they live for the moment, with little hope for tomorrow.

Are these people money obsessed? Yes, it appears so, but only, in my opinion, because they have none. Debate: Does money rule the world as Grandma Lambe used to say? People are freer when they have no money. They want to grab at any fun and cherish it. I've also decided that Americans are the worst people on the planet. I sat beside them at the Zócalo. They whinged more than British people and only talked about why Americans are better than everyone. Their behaviour brings these words to mind: 'Positive experience of another culture relies on the travellers' participation.' I certainly agree, and am up for it.

21 August 1997

I have a really dicky tummy. In other words, 'me tums off'. I could shit through the eye of a needle. Must have been the coffee at the hotel, or maybe the mezcal! I have to tell Prince Charles that Herman from Oaxaca is coming to stay. More on that later.

I sat in the middle of the desert in a VW Beetle. The only sound was the occasional car driving along the road about two miles away. An eagle flew overhead, and something was squeaking in the cacti. It was peaceful, but at the same time I had an uneasy feeling, as if predators were watching our every move. I got out, sat on the ground and ate some bread, convinced I'd be stung or bitten.

I got back in the car! The sky was vast and ended at the mountains that provided the walls of the valley. Never did I imagine I'd be in such a situation. It was truly amazing. There was nothing there but three of us, a VW and miles of desert. Only for the intrepid conqueror.

Mountains were silhouetted in the dark sky, and a single star watched over us. The moon had yet to show its face. There must have been a reason for me being there.

We drove around some villages in the Central Valleys. I felt quite guilty as my camera flashed, like it was an invasion of their privacy. These are detached from any form of western culture, and they are treated like exhibits: a stopping point for the tourist industry.

Darkness, like the curtains of a stage, rolled over the valley. It was time to leave.

On the way back we stopped at Santa María del Tule for a walk. We saw a couple of humongous trees with railings around them and a small amusement park. Some village street-kids follow us for a while, whistling and cheering, before losing interest. We eventually made our way back to the hotel by way of the very annoying one-way system. My stomach has been dodgy all day. Marco suggested pretzels and cola. Please! Make me feel better!

Music creates scenarios, I think. *The Doors* soundtrack and *Carmina Burana* in the middle of the desert was particularly amazing. This morning I phoned home. Papa Totten died. Tomorrow I will light a candle in the cathedral for him. It's a strange feeling. Images of when I was younger flash past. Poor old Papa!

The guy I mentioned earlier—Herman—met Prince Charles when he was in Oaxaca. Herman is a Mariachi, and Prince Charles invited him to stay in England. Hum! He is saving his money and hopes to go soon. I'll have to pass on the message!

I've realised my greatest fear is failure. Anything else I can handle, but not that!

22 August 1997

My stomach was feeling better, so we decided to explore the surrounding valley. The German boys met some people from their home village who came in the car with us. We drove off the main road about two kilometres down a dirt track, where we stopped to eat. Farmers herding goats and oxen passed. We walked on up the side of the hill to look for some rocks. It was very peaceful. A golden eagle flew overhead. I found a scorpion under a rock—small, but nevertheless a scorpion—and a gnu-shaped stone. Very cool!

The 'group' has increased in number, but I feel more alone. I am looking forward to meeting people in Zipolite. Money is going to be a problem, as there is no further Amex. Maybe I'll be able to buy some more travellers' cheques if we get back to Oaxaca in time. (It's very disappointing, but I can't expect people to speak another language for my benefit.)

We visited another archaeological site: Dainzú (a Zapotec site about twenty kilometres from Oaxaca—small but interesting, with very basic information).

I got to Amex three minutes after the cashier closed. Shit! I'll have to wait for Belize or Guatemala. So I'm forced to change my last travellers' cheques after only eight days. Deary me! Too bad, but 'when will I ever be in Mexico again?' is the best attitude.

We bought bus tickets and then went to a great little vegetarian restaurant where the food was clean and wholesome, which cheered me up immensely—three courses at only 22 pesos. BARG! It was time to say goodbye to Axel and Blanca, as we set off to catch the bus from Pochulta to Zipolite.

23 August 1997

Zip-iddy-doo-dah! We arrived at 4.30 a.m., after a journey through the jungle. I was sitting in a hammock outside Honchos, and I felt like I was in a Pepsi advert. There were some really 'chill toons' playing, and a light sea breeze blew through the cabana. Everyone was sitting doing nothing in particular. Birds squawking from coconut palms could be heard, and an occasional taxi drove down the dust track. Could this be real? Yes! Yes! Yes! I felt the most relaxed I've ever felt. All I needed was a big red parrot on the roof of the cabana. The thought persisted.

My next thought was "Ants will rule the world." Why? Is it because they move in armies? Perhaps! Extreme heat, like there is here, is too much for most creatures, but it is a friend to the ant. When most insects succumb to dehydration caused by the excessive heat, the ant comes out to forage for 'lunch'. Thinking of these things as I swung in my hammock watching the world go by, I dozed.

I awoke to the sound of the waves. I walked down the beach. The waves grew louder and louder. My feet sunk into the soft white sands. There were only bamboo cabanas and hammocks in sight, and it was surrounded by jungle and rugged coastline. I took my first dip in the warm and powerful waves of the Pacific Ocean. Hallelujah!

Evening brought a major problem: mosquitoes! You'd need a metal suit to stop them. I had a very uncomfortable night's sleep, and woke up with so many bites, that I looked like I had measles. The little bastards. I went downstairs and had breakfast: Kellogg's cornflakes and bananas. WOW! What a place! After breakfast I went for a swim before going back to chill out at the cabana for the rest of the day. We met quite a lot of interesting people—some English as well.

When we went for our late-afternoon swim, a Mexican trickster decided it would be great fun to bury my sandals on the beach. Ha-ha! Thinking at first that he'd stolen them, and feeling macho, I ran up the beach after him. When I did catch up with him, much to my embarrassment, I saw that the sandals on his feet were completely different to mine. Puzzled, I walked back to where I'd been sitting and I saw a strap poking out of the sand. Lo and behold, he'd buried them—most likely to collect later. Not outwitted, I returned to the cabana.

Johnny's Sandals which got 'buried' in the sand

We went to eat at the same place as the night before: spaghetti marinara. Bueno! Lots of fresh fish. Just think, two hours ago it was alive and swimming.

The girls from the cabana came to sit with us: one French, one American. We arranged to meet them later at a party on the beach. We walked the length of the beach. No party was to be found! It was incredibly dark, and the only sound was the White Horses crashing onto the beach. We found the party on the way back and realised the problem: we'd set off 'untrendily' early, only to arrive 'fashionably' late.

At the party, I spoke English, without drawing breath, to Alex, a girl from Stirling University. They were on the way to San Cristóbal, so maybe we'll meet them there. Finally, we adjourned to our cabana, thoroughly exhausted and drunk.

Days seem to pass you by; it is as if time is standing still. Days spent hanging around in hammocks, out drinking in the *posadas* (inns) or diving through the waves on the beach. Have to do something tomorrow.

25 August 1997

Woke up and had breakfast and a morning swim—the perfect way to start a day. We got ourselves together and went to search out a boat to take us to see the dolphins and turtles that Carrie and Alex had told us about, then we headed off in a *colectivo* to Mazunte. The *colectivo* was like a pickup truck with a roof, that you stood up or sat down in—great fun.

Mazunte was even quieter and more unspoilt than Zipolite. There were no boats to be seen on the shore, so 'Captain Johnny' decided to lead his troops around the rocks, feeling smooth and confident with his new beach trousers and camera. Inevitably, we were drenched and forced to retreat and climb the cliffs to the 'safe' jungle. Convinced I would be eaten alive, I ran terrified through undergrowth, I'm sure, never before seen or touched by man. I reached the edge of the 'jungle' after several small panic attacks. I had only ten feet of long grass to get through before the safety of the beach. Maybe an easy dash, but not in sandals and turned-up, wet trousers. Of course, I made it to the beach and threw myself into the sea to clear away any insects or debris left over from the forest. 'Smooth Johnny' no longer felt so smooth, especially when two surfers turned up by the rocks we had just turned back from. Didums! These things are not supposed to happen in paradise.

However, major highlight! On the beach there was a small boat with some fishermen who were easily persuaded to take us out on the boat to see some marine life for 50 pesos each. Quite a bargain!

We gave the boat a traditional shove-off from the dock using bamboo sticks and manpower, and we set off out to sea. Where we were going was up to them.

Are they genuine? and other thoughts entered my mind as I watched the Pacific Coast pass by—kilometres of virgin-white sand and coconut palms surrounded completely by jungle. It took an effort for me to see the reality of the situation.

Now, there was a guy standing in the stern of the boat doing what I thought were Tai Chi exercises. Then he bolted from the boat and went missing underwater for what seemed like an eternity but was only a few minutes. He surfaced on the opposite side of the boat, driving a sea turtle. Jan and I jumped into the depths of the Pacific Ocean to enjoy the transportation of this amazing creature ourselves. It was like steering a car. I plunged under with the turtle, and it swam through the depths of the sea, passing snakes and other sea creatures as we went.

No sign of Jaws though. Phew! We got back into the boat then continued a few more times until we became 'expert' turtle-spotters and were allowed to try to catch them ourselves. To no avail! All too soon the hour was over, and to the shore. Delighted with our day's adventure with Leonardo, Michaelangelo, Donatello and Raphael, back on shore we headed for the nearest cabana for a refreshing bottle of grapefruit juice served by huge great Mexican women. We laughed, hysterically for twenty minutes, not exchanging a word.

After a swim in a riptide that could have pulled down an elephant, we returned by *colectivo* to Zipolite.

25 August 1997

I am beginning to completely unwind and just enjoy being in Mexico, but soon we'll have to move from paradise. Well, probably in a couple of days. I'll have to miss a few places unfortunately, but I think it's best to take in the atmosphere and not rush around like a Japanese tourist.

Back at the Cabana El Niños things were much as usual. The English girls had left, and we had a relaxing dinner with a French girl and a quite-ordinary American guy. Maybe Americans are not too bad! Spaghetti carbonara all round. Fortunately, we were able to put it on the bill, as funds were low. Hung about in our hammocks afterwards, until drifted to sleep surrounded by lizards, rats, mice, a wasp nest and, of course, the humming of the killer mosquitoes from hell.

26 August 1997

We decided over a spliff to wait until the next day before leaving. We made for the *casa de cambio* (exchange house) in the bright midday sunlight, the heat excruciating—probably the hottest I've ever experienced. It would be impossible to hold down a full-time job here, due to heat exhaustion. I look forward to it being a bit cooler in San Cristóbal Highlands—not that I particularly want to leave the beach.

After a breakfast of fruit salad and choco-milk, and being flogged a silver bracelet at the beach, the morning swim made me realise the pure joy of being in the sea and being in touch with the elements: the fresh warm air, the powerful crashing waves, the soft sand and the fiery sun. If I could float with less hassle, I would have stayed in forever. Maybe it's the Pisces coming out. We had spent a while tidying and sweeping the cabana, so the luxury of a clean cabin on our return made me feel fresh and eager.

I'm in one of the bars along the beach, sitting here watching the sea. Life has never been so good. The only thing is, it would be nice to have the guys and gals from home to play with on the beach and drink with at night. But then again, it is great to have a break from all that and to just be myself among people from the rest of the world, with no expectations or preconceptions as to how I should be, etc.

It's a very rewarding feeling to travel alone. I am enjoying a break from Jan and Marco too. They're great, and very relaxed to travel with, but I'd go mad if I had to spend all day every day with them, bearing in mind that only a short while ago they were complete strangers.

The most exhilarating moment when travelling is that moment when you get off the plane and reality bites. I'm beginning to get a bit down about my return, but also excited. I keep imagining that moment when I meet my parents at the airport, and then stepping into the doorway of Albion Road. It will be different. No Vern in the house to get pissed off with, and vice versa, but I'll miss him. He's only across the road. Little Al is moving in: a calming influence, more outgoing and something of a wanderer. Neil will have changed after his father's death; Steven, much the same but travelled; Bertie, hopefully new for 1997/98, without Dominic; and as for Paul, who knows what effect his travels would have had on him. I wonder what they are doing now in Europe. Poor Marcella, Vern and Matt probably have exams as I speak. I'd love to have them all here for a day. We'd be 'The Ones'.

Lovis just came and sat down next to me, but left when I told him I was enjoying being on my own. I hope I didn't sound too rude. I think he understood. Zipolite is a place for beautiful people; you have to be someone. It can be annoying talking to people who have been everywhere and done everything, especially when that is the extent of their conversation and I am sitting here covered in 'fresher's' mosquito bites—forty-three to be precise, and those are only the ones on my arms and legs. (I prefer not to know about the ones on other parts of my body.)

Perfection is a very difficult thing to find. If achieved, it would be very difficult to deal with anything else afterwards. At this moment, I feel that I have found the next best thing, excluding the discomfort of sleeping in a hammock, the vampire mosquitoes from hell that can bite through steel and the odd coked-up fucker who walks around thinking he is God's gift to humanity. I hate the fact that I notice these imperfections, as they are all completely normal and should just be accepted. I *do* accept them! Happiness only comes at a price, which when taken into consideration is an incredible bargain. Marco says that in Europe everyone should be happy but …

Marco and Jan arrived, and we walked along the beach to meet Lovis for dinner. We each chose a different fish dish to share. The fish was very good indeed. Absolutely! We went back to El Niños before heading to El Disco. What a place! NOT! We met some Germans and danced. Lovis had some very cool moves. What a tiger! We left the disco, ready for a good night's sleep, having danced all night. TRASHED!

27 August 1997

Woke up feeling slightly rough. It was time to leave Zipolite and the hammock-lying days. However, the thought of a comfortable hotel, milder weather, fewer mosquitoes and no sand made it less painful. We said farewell to our new friends. We had only spent a short time with them, but it felt like a little family had sprung up in the cabana. Having not yet left, I was missing it already. We went to the usual restaurant on the beach and watched the waves over the usual carbonara and choco-milk. We set off in unbearable heat to Tecolutla. Fortunately, we got the last three tickets for the evening, eleven-hour bus ride to San Cristóbal de las Casas.

We had a last swing in our hammocks before the taxi picked us up at 9 p.m. to take us to the bus station. I do hope I come back here one day.

Oh yeah! The taxi we took to the bus station was horrific: Formula 1 racing around the winding coast. I felt sure we'd had it.

The bus was late, but after half an hour of *Apollo 13*, I somehow drifted off to sleep. I woke at some unearthly hour, when we had to change buses before a sickly journey through the mountains to San Cristóbal. We met a Canadian girl called Shareen who asked if she could join our quest for a B&B. We found a room with two doubles for 20 pesos per night. Pokey as it was, we didn't complain. Anything was better than the hammock with rats at El Niños.

We set off with Shareen to the Zócalo to find somewhere to eat and get some cash. I wore myself ragged running from bank to bank. Finally, I resigned myself to ringing the emergency line in England, to be informed that it was impossible to obtain cash with an Amex card. Wonderful! I would have to go to Tuxtla Gutiérrez, the capital of the state of Chiapas, where the Amex representative would help me out. It was a miserable day, walking around markets with no spending power. Not much fun! I convinced the 'crew' to go to a bar that accepted my credit card. I could do nothing else. We ate and drank. My second official tequila went down with more pain than the first. It was time to pay the gastronomical bill: 210 pesos. We'll be washing up dishes for the rest of our lives.

I'm sure you are beginning to see a pattern in my holiday experiences: budgeting my funds and finding places to eat that were good value. Food is very important to me. I like to cook and eat good food. Even as a nine-year-old child I got into trouble at a Cubs camp when I told the leader she should not be allowed to be in charge of a group of children, as her food was disgusting. In fact, I said it was abuse to feed children such food. Needless to say, I had to apologise, under threat of being sent home, which I did. I was a bit ashamed afterwards.

Having had a bit of a blow-out, we now had to look for an inexpensive evening meal. We found a restaurant, Paris-Mexico, where a decent and very reasonable menu was on offer for 25 pesos, including a margarita. Nice hot bread rolls with garlic butter, a very fresh salsa, followed by soup Aztec (a Mexican speciality with chillies, cheese, avocado and tacos (probably the Mexican equivalent of croutons)) for starters. The main course was a rather dull fish with indistinguishable vegetables in a tomato sauce. Filling but unremarkable. The dessert was a crème caramel followed by a coffee—not bad.

Feeling replete and tired, we made for the bar next door. There was some interesting modern art on the walls and an amazing live bongo and percussion set with three guys. Their sound was incredible. The bar was jam-packed with travellers. Two-for-the-price-of-one beer was also a bonus—although I only managed one myself. The band left and the disco began. We'd had very little sleep the night before because of the journey.

I had to go to Tuxtla the next day. Jan, Marco and Shareen had arranged a five-hour tour around the lanes, on horses, at 9 a.m. We went back to the B&B for an early night.

Jan was sick—most likely the result of too much tequila. Shareen was plastered, having consumed four large margaritas. I was beginning to feel the side-effects of the chloroquine antimalarial tablets. I'm sure they are not doing me any good, but I have no choice but to take them. After a brief lesson on German and Canadian philosophy (the Canadian being mostly anti-American), we all went to sleep in the two double beds. I got to share with Shareen.

PS I don't think there is much to do here in San Cristóbal—it's a smaller version of Oaxaca—but you can arrange excursions to other places.

Jan has just accused the Stone Roses of being Britpop. I said, "The Stone Roses were around before Britpop was a twinkle in your father's eye." They didn't understand!

Jan woke up several times in the night to be sick. I think once over the bed and once over Marco.

2 August 1997

I'm now sitting in Pizza Romani in Tuxtla City eating probably the most disgusting pizza I have ever encountered. I'd ordered a medium, expecting a nice fresh crispy base, like Pizza Express … but not here. It looks like ham, mushroom and cheese on shortbread. The salsa is also pretty grotesque, but I have an hour to wait before the Amex office opens. Just my luck! This pizza is lasting far too long. I hope it has a lot of nutritional value, because it hasn't much else to offer. The choco-milk is shit too: sickly sweet.

Today started with an unbearable breakfast in Stan Cristóbal; the curse on the food has continued all day. Never mind. I'll live. I hope!

I went to a church to say some prayers. It seemed like a nice idea. Then I took the 11.30 bus to Tuxtla and slept all the way there. On my way to the Tourist Information Office, I passed a huge rally. Fortunately, my instincts served me well and I found the Amex before the Tourist Information Office.

Roll on four o'clock, so that I can leave this place. The others are having a lovely day horse riding in the mountains, while I'm stuck in the worst place in Mexico. It reminds me of that place Mark Mangan took us to in Germany: Dessau—concrete, bad food and nothing happening. Maybe I'll write a poem about Tuxtla later today. That's all you can do about these places: turn them into a reason as opposed to a place. There are an awful lot of Mexicans here, would you believe? Three slices of pizza to go. Where's Josh (the dog) when you need him? The Amex man who is just about to save my life is now sitting in the restaurant. I refuse to leave a tip. They wrap the rest of the pizza from hell up for me to take home. DAM! I left a tip. They were so proud of the pizza, and I didn't want to be rude.

MISSION ACCOMPLISHED! US $300. Now back to San Cristóbal. The shits have returned! I was seriously fretting for the health of my trousers, so dived into a place for an Aqua Mineral and the use of the toilet. Thank God!

Hello! It's the enemy! I'm in a really bad mood and need to be somewhere on my own for a bit. I want to play squash and get rid of all this tension. Today has been shit all round, and I am going mad. I don't know why at all. Maybe I'm overtired and sick to death making an effort to communicate with people who don't speak any English at all, and if they do, it is with a fucking annoying accent. I want a room of my own with a carpet and a TV where I can unwind. I feel that I've let myself down by not doing enough on my own and becoming reliant on other people. But maybe it's just today. I got back to San Cristóbal ready to hit anyone trying to sell me anything. No fucking gratis! Maybe I'm going through a mid-trip crisis. To be honest, I'm just a bit bored and find San Cristóbal to be too much like Oaxaca to be at all exciting. I'm stressed out with buses and people. I'm restless to have my own adventure, but when I suggest this, it is vetoed. Probably fear. That fucking tape which sounds like a fucking combination of Morrissey and A-ha is playing. I am going insane!

I tried to phone home, but no joy.

Another day went past with me feeling excluded and exiled from my own nationality. Shit! I sound like a nationalistic cunt, but ho-hum. I want to run away. I've just had another shit meal, which fucked me off. A microwave hot dog! Tomorrow I'm going to have to go on another bus and spend more time waiting. I need to assert myself more and really be alone. On the other hand, I'm sure the grass is always greener. Hopefully, tomorrow things will have changed. What a lovely ending to my first book. I feel completely uninspired and unenthusiastic. I want to leave this fucking shithole of a hotel, which is like a prison. Four people within four metres. I'm getting nowhere. GIVE ME SPACE! CHILL, JOHNNY!

'Give me Space Chill Johnny'. After a bad day 29/08/1997

I don't know why I stuck this in. It was a shit journey. It rained all day and it stressed me out. Mind you, on the bright side, the scenery was incredible: the mist and the clouds crowning the alpine mountains. I also got to read plenty of *The Lord of the Rings*. Merry and Pippin are safe! What's up with Frodo? I'll read on. I'm feeling much better already, having whinged myself dry. Tomorrow will be a nice day. It fucking better be! Early start!

CTG tickets to Tuxtla and Las Casa 29/08/97

I was travelling, so was unaware that Princess Diana had died until I saw the billboards of her funeral—which would take place on 6 September—in Mexico City. I didn't see the sea of flowers around Buckingham Palace, nor did I witness the outpouring of grief. I am so far away, which made it seem unreal. Nick told me afterwards that he'd come in from school with Mark to find Mum and Dad in tears as they watched the funeral on television. He knew immediately what the problem was, but his friend's response was, "What's wrong?" Perhaps he'd never seen his parents cry, or maybe he was just totally unaware of current affairs. Sixteen-year-old boys!

Chapter 6

Johnny 1998–2007 by Mona Lambe

Johnny was a fair-haired little thing (only nine pounds and ten ounces), kicking and struggling, and determined to do it all by himself. I was so relieved to get a boy after the two girls, and what joy he brought with him. A great sleeper and a versatile feeder: easy to breast or bottle feed.

John used to sit up in bed, watching him being fed. Then he put Johnny on his chest and let him sleep there for a while. When he was older, Johnny would wake up in the evening and be happy to sit quietly with us. He did not enjoy the cot, so we put him in a big double bed, where he could play with his Fisher Price garage before going to sleep. A good companion and interested in everything. His favourite pastimes were making fruit salad, drawing, painting, cutting out, listening to stories and music—the things he would enjoy for the rest of his life.

Johnny could, 'talk for Ireland'; in fact, he kissed the Blarney Stone when he was about four months old on a family tour around the south-west of Ireland. During this same tour he cut his first tooth.

We left Northern Ireland because of the troubles, and we went to Oakville, Ontario.

It was home-schooling for Johnny, as he couldn't start school until he was six. He had lessons on the computer at the library and joined a gymnastics club, while reading, writing, colouring and cooking were the order of the day with Mum.

We returned to the UK, Hove actually. Johnny went into the first year at Balfour School. Separation anxiety kicked in, but he was very happy with his first teacher, Mrs Saunders. She recognised Johnny's thoughtfulness and creativity, and she was happy to let him follow her around the classroom because he did so quietly and was never intrusive—a useful trait later on in life when he was filming.

It was a struggle to get him to school. Every day he'd say, "I'm not going!" Finally ,I thought of a 'stress day', as my sister, Emma, called it. "Let's have a quiet day at home baking some butterfly buns."

The root of the problem was bullying. Johnny, like a lot of children, had 'playground terror'. I, too, had experienced this feeling, but I could always call on my brothers for protection. John taught Johnny to make a fist. After this, Johnny seemed more confident, knowing he had our support. I explained the situation to the teacher. She'd had complaints from other parents. Pity a meeting hadn't been called to let us all—parents and children—know that the problem was being dealt with.

The big bad world of reality entered the life of a happy, gentle little boy. Fear and insecurity had arrived, and I believe he battled with these for the rest of his life.

At junior school he became something of an entertainer in the playground, as he didn't like football, the only other option at playtimes. Party invitations were plentiful, and he enjoyed camping out with his friends at home and at their homes, just as he loved the freedom of our camping holidays in France.

However, every day it was still a struggle to get him to school, and he and his father were constantly at loggerheads, vying for my undivided attention. He went to boarding school when he was eleven.

Johnny was delighted to be embarking on a new adventure. Before long, boredom with the restrictions and daily routine set in, and after a year he was ready to come home. Reading through his letters, I can see how painful it all was for him. He would become a very single-minded, resilient, independent individual. Johnny made friends and adjusted quite well, but still suffered the first three weeks of every term.

Dirty Dancing was a family favourite—a feel-good movie. We adored the soundtrack. It became a habit for Johnny, before returning to school, to say, "Let's go into the dining room and dance to our music, Mum." My favourite was 'Hungry Eyes', but Johnny's favourite was 'I Had the Time of My Life'.

Brutally honest—rude even as a child—smoking terrified him, and he once broke up a new packet of cigarettes and threw them into the bin. He had boundless energy and liked to confront his fears or challenge himself, like the day he deliberately stepped out in front of a car at the school gates.

Johnny was a boy with a multitude of talents: a sensation seeker who wanted to experience all aspects of life. He was eager to leave Coleraine, but at the same time he was sad, and he said, "I will always be an 'Instonian'."

He enjoyed Brighton College and made some lifelong friends there, travelling with them in France and Europe. He immersed himself in history, English and art. Some good work and results took him to Manchester University to read History of Art. He gained his BA (Hons) despite part-time jobs, academic work and playing hard with the friends he loved.

He told me in later years that he regretted going to Manchester instead of accepting his place on the Art Foundation Course. Johnny needed to get away from home rules, my love and his father's fear. He said, "Dad wants me to sit in a buggy for the rest of my life." Johnny sensed our anxiety and overprotectiveness. Two incidents created John's paranoia: one was waking up to find that Johnny, the baby he cherished and adored, had slipped down off his chest under the bed covers, and two was being paralysed with fear as he watched Johnny running down the driveway towards open gates and a main road, into the path of two cars coming in opposite directions, shouting "Daddy, Daddy, I want to go with you". A heart-stopping sight. Little things change our lives as well as big things, and we are all touched by our childhood.

Parting from Johnny when he went to infant school, Coleraine then university all brought tears of anguish from me.

The trip to Manchester, with all Johnny's precious belongings, was the first of many such trips with an overloaded car. A nomadic life, he moved from a student flat to a house in Manchester. The constant throughout his life was his family and friends who supported him even after they'd all moved on from university.

It was goodbye Manchester, hello London!

Graduation Day University of Manchester

Chapter 7

London

Hareth, his best, dearest and most loyal friend, told me later that he and Johnny helped each other to survive.

One of Johnny's many jobs was in Borough Market. On Christmas Eve he arrived at Brighton Station with a goose under his arm, recipe and all. The roast goose was Boxing Day lunch with the gang—an unforgettable memory. Johnny found working as a runner interesting and worked on Jooles Holland—Young Jazz Musician of the Year—with a dear friend, Kate Mirren. At the same time, he was working with an agency that recruited technical people for films. He told me after one job interview that it was like being interviewed by the 'Two Fat Ladies', our favourite TV chefs at that time. His lean and hungry looks would touch the heart of any two fat ladies. He got the job.

He felt relaxed with them and was able to display all his qualities: funny, clever and talented. The downside was walking their Great Dane. A sight to behold, no doubt.

He became more confident, but it was a stop gap, and the money was an insult and impossible to live on. It was very disheartening—no money, no home, no creative opportunities.

He was a great pound-stretcher and could pick up top-quality clothes in charity shops. He couldn't afford paints, so he used old glossy magazines and produced some delightful collages.

Always needing to be busy, he used what watercolours he had to make Mother's Day cards, and he did a painting of the Seven Sisters for Cheryl when she got married in 1999.

Watercolour on Hessian by Johnny Lambe: 'Seven Sisters'. A Wedding present for Cheryl

Johnny came home for the bank holiday at the end of August 2001. He looked emaciated. "I'm going to New York. I've booked my ticket," he said.

How on earth will he survive in New York when he could barely subsist in London? I thought.

We sat down in the breakfast room to have a chat. "Johnny, one thing I have always admired about you is your ability to listen to advice and then make a decision. Go to New York, but stay at home for a while; save up a bit of money and then go."

Johnny didn't say much, but off he went to the travel agent to see if he could change his flight. He also searched Brighton for something to do. His flight to New York was booked for 9/11!

Instead, he went to film school in Brighton—the beginning of his love affair with film-making.

This page and the following page.
Jack Cardiff visits the Film School in Brighton where Johnny is a student.

CAP THAT! Top cameraman Jack Cardiff, 87, was happy to apply his expertise for free to a production by first-time film-makers

Jack of movie trade gets in the picture

YOU could almost picture the cigarette dangling from Bette Davis' lips and Humphrey Bogart leaning against the wall.

Film noir had come to a bedroom in Sussex and it had that authentic feeling suggesting the presence of a real Hollywood legend.

Bogie would probably have felt at home as a group of first-time film-makers recreated Fifties LA under the guidance of a true film great, Jack Cardiff.

The 87-year-old Oscar-winning cinematographer has filmed stars, including Marilyn Monroe, Katherine Hepburn and Laurence Olivier.

He has worked with directors such as Alfred Hitchcock and David Lean.

Last year he was the toast

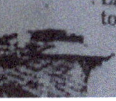

SUCCESS: Humphrey Bogart in The African

PICTURE: RICHARD GRANGE   70721-2

ACTION MEN: Members of the Flamingo Blues crew

of Hollywood after becoming the first cameraman to receive the Lifetime Achievement Award at the Oscars.

On arriving in Sussex, he switched the bright lights of LA for a bedroom in Lewes to work for free on a low-budget film by a fledgling Brighton-based company.

the script, he immediately offered to lend a hand.

Jack said: "I am enjoying myself tremendously. I'm not getting paid so the great thing is I can't be fired. The director wrote the script as well. I think it's marvellous and has a lot of promise.

"There is a lot of enthusi-

retire. He said: "I think to drop dead on the set would be the perfect way to go."

Director Robbi said: "Working with Jack has been one of the best days of my life. I have learned more on this set than you could ever imagine. The man is extraordinary, a charming person and a perfect gentleman."

The first scenes of the £30,000 film Flamingo Blues were shot at South Street, Lewes, home of one of the film's producers, Tom Leeburn. Tom, 22, said: 'I think Jack was attracted to the film because it's not set in the London gangster world and hasn't got Hugh Grant in it. It's extremely inspiring and reassuring to have him on set.

"We've had people phoning up and offering to work on it for free because Jack is working on it. We're not making a student film, I suppose I would call it a post-student film. We have secured a third of the budget but are still look-

...mingo Blues crew

...script, he immediately ...red to lend a hand.

...ack said: "I am enjoying ...self tremendously. I'm not ...ting paid so the great thing ...can't be fired. The director ...ote the script as well. I ...nk it's marvellous and has ...t of promise.

There is a lot of enthusi... ...at Brighton Film School ..., you never know, there ... be another Spielberg ...dy in the ranks."

...ck won an Oscar in 1947 ...his cinematography on ...k Narcissus.

...e started out as a child ...e star but moved behind ...scenes, becoming a cam... ...operator on the first Tech... ...lor film made in England. ...e filmed his finest work in ...orties, including The Red ...s. In 1951 he helped Bog... ...win his only Oscar with ...African Queen.

...ck, who has also directed ..., has more projects in the ...line and no plans to

...charming person and ... ...fect gentleman."

The first scenes of the £30,000 film Flamingo Blues were shot at South Street, Lewes, home of one of the film's producers, Tom Leeburn. Tom, 22, said: "I think Jack was attracted to the film because it's not set in the London gangster world and hasn't got Hugh Grant in it. It's extremely inspiring and reassuring to have him on set.

"We've had people phoning up and offering to work on it for free because Jack is working on it. We're not making a student film, I suppose I would call it a post-student film. We have secured a third of the budget but are still looking for more funding."

Fellow film-maker Matthew Chadwick, 20, said: "He knows what he's doing and we can combine that with all the new talent coming through."

Johnny Lambe, 25, found himself on set with Jack on only his second day at the film school. He said: "I feel privileged and I'm going to grab the opportunity to watch him at work."

The film could be finished by the end of February, in time to secure a slot on the festival circuit.

Barbara Davidson
barbara.davidson
@theargus.co.uk

Tranquillity for a while. No money worries, a room of his own, food on the table, and to top it all, meeting interesting people and learning exciting new things. A result of this was 'Midnight Blues'. It all seemed to be falling into place, and Johnny had time to do some writing. He met Marta there, and they became good friends.

Chapter 8
New York, New York
2001

I have been home for ten days now, and I am eating well and feeling less anxious, but still not getting much sleep. My 'thought' for today, 9 September 2001, is this: sometimes you just have to move the piano.

I went to bed at midnight on 10 September and was awakened from a deep sleep at 1.52 a.m. on the 11th.

I was disorientated at first. I thought I was in New York and was incredibly raring to go! I shall do as planned and go to view the city from its highest point: The World Trade Centre, Tower One.

I took the lift to the top and stepped onto the viewing gallery. Hannah, my university friend who did a great Elvis impression for us at Sunday lunch in the garden, was here. This tower moved more than I'd imagined it would. 'It's vertigo,' I thought, or jet lag setting in! The swaying got even stronger. I felt a bit concerned. "I think we should get the lift back down now, Hannah," I said. This movement was not just jet lag or vertigo; the place was moving a little bit more than is to be desired. We walked to the lift. Only four people inside. We got in. The door closed. Suddenly the swaying sensation became that of falling and tumbling through the air for what seemed like forever. A bang and crash!

I couldn't move, but I was still alive. Hannah was no longer with me, but Kate was lying dead beside me, sprawled next to the other people in the lift.

I was fully awake now. I got out of bed, turned on the light, walked up and down the stairs to clear my head then lay down and drifted off to sleep.

I got up out of bed at lunchtime, had a bite to eat then took the dog for a walk. When I got back home from the walk I decided to watch *The Goonies* on video—a way for me to escape into childhood fantasy. I do this a lot now while I await Monday's departure to the Big Apple, where I will attempt to find my future, whatever that should be.

The telephone rang. Jane's voice was at the other end of the line. "Hello, Johnny. I am so glad you are not in New York. Have you seen the breaking news on TV? A hijacked plane has flown into the World Trade Centre, causing massive explosions in the city. I am worried about you going to New York. Go and see the coverage on TV. I'll speak to you later."

The United States of America appeared to be under attack from terrorists. The World Trade Centre was in flames. I watched as another aeroplane flew into Tower Two. One after the other, the Twin Towers collapsed. Manhattan was a disaster zone as a result of the worst attack of terrorism the world had ever seen. I was supposed to arrive in New York yesterday afternoon, but changed my flight in order to enjoy another week of recuperation. Had everything gone to plan, I would perhaps have been somewhere around The World Trade Centre today. Someone up there is looking after me. A text from EWJ said, "Johnny, you are a lucky man. God is on your side."

14 September 2001

Three days of endless news about Tuesday's atrocities. My mind, as is that of all those who inhabit televisual societies, was paralysed with horror, yet somehow alert to the continuous stream of horrific wrongs we witnessed this week. Is New York still the place of my dreams? I have postponed my date of departure. I wait in a state of flux. Is my 'American dream' still a plausible option or will an imminent war force me to rethink? *Que sera*. Fortunately, I could relax in the comfort of home, tucked safely away in the south-east of England.

My first reaction was, I think that I should go anyway—stubborn and independent in the face of such catastrophic events. Life must go on. The world won't stop now. I filled the next few days with a frenzy of writing.

TRUE LOVE—A Three-Minute Short

Two very old and very stooped people, living a drab and lonely existence, get up every morning and go about their lives as best they can. They shuffle around their homes, drink some tea then go out to do a bit of shopping. They are splashed with water from passing cars and meet each other in the street, but are unable to make eye contact, as they are bent almost double.

Then, in a supermarket, while looking at the same brand of tea—Yorkshire—they look up and get their first fleeting glimpse of each other. They glance up again, and their eyes linger a little longer.

They look down at their baskets, which contain the same uninspiring staples: milk, tea, sugar and bread. They look up again, and they smile. TRUE LOVE!

The couple shuffle off together—no words spoken.

We hear music in the background—sombre notes of the violin—interspersed with the familiar sounds of everyday life: cars, kettles whistling, alarm clocks going off, buses passing, the ping of a cash register, traffic lights beeping, doors slamming.

BLACKOUT ESCAPE

Two young men have just dined in a relatively expensive restaurant. They set their wine glasses down at the end of the meal. A waiter wearing black and white brings the bill on a silver tray and sets it down in front of one of the young men, who presumes the other is paying. He slides the bill across the table in the direction of his friend, as he is unable to do so. They jiggle the coins in their pockets, which they then take out and display in the open palms of their hands, indicating the lack of funds. PANIC!

Then ... POWER CUT! They see each other by the light from the flickering candle. Each man nods decisively, meaning 'Let's run!' The candle is snuffed out between a wet forefinger and thumb. DARKNESS!

HERO

Hero arrives at school to find himself in the middle of a brawl between the school bully and a younger pupil. Bully is about to deliver a punch, when Hero steps in and gets a black eye. Teacher comes round the corner, and seeing our bemused Hero, reprimands him and apparently threatens punishment. Bully escapes, smiling. Hero walks off to the toilets to clean himself up and is jeered at by a few smokers who flick their fag ends at him and promptly leave.

A cigarette lands at Hero's feet. Then Teacher appears, looking down at the burning cigarette then up at Hero, who shakes his head in denial. Teacher then hands out a punishment slip, assuming Hero is the guilty party.

Hero is late getting to class and is again reprimanded, while Bully sniggers happily.

The bell rings; it is lunchtime, and the class leaves to eat lunch in the cafeteria, leaving their bags in a pile outside the lunch room. Lunch is the usual bun fight. Bully jeers and throws food at Hero, which hits him in the face. Hero cleans the food from his face with a sweeping gesture, and some of it hits the teacher in the face. Hero is reprimanded again!

When he leaves the lunchroom, Bully rifles through the boys' bags. He takes out an exercise book and then swaggers off happily to copy the homework as is usual.

Hero searches his schoolbag for his homework in vain. Where can it be? Teacher thinks Hero has fucked up again. No homework!

IDENTITY

I am born. I roam the earth, visible to others but invisible to myself. I identify as Dancer! A real identity, a perceived identity or only a figment of my unquantifiable imagination.

In a white space, with only my thoughts for company, I feel both isolation and desolation.

I try to find confidence through confrontation, exploration and creative expression, but in the end there is no resolution—just a feeling of confusion, futility and emptiness.

NO IDENTITY! I am unable to communicate verbally, as I have no spoken language. My reflection in a mirror tells me I am of the human race, but beyond that there is nothing, and before that, empty space. I search for identity by imitation, but still I have no name, and no name seems to fit. Emotions wash in torrents over me, and thinking is something I like to do a lot when these feelings are structured. I would like to tell my story.

The claustrophobic who is confined to a small space and is worried about the dangers he or she might encounter in the real world is also an agoraphobic (afraid of the outdoors). He exemplifies the conflict between the safety of seclusion versus the need to experience external reality.

QVC, the shopping channel, which to me represents Barbara Kirchner's (1978) idea that 'I shop, therefore I am'. Can ownership of an object improve the quality of life or bring happiness? I say no. We are not defined by our worldly goods or by one specific incident or aspect of our life.

17 September 2001

I am supposed to be on a plane to New York, but instead I sit in a café in Kensington Gardens, Brighton, thinking about icons.

What is an icon? This thought has been uppermost in our minds since the destruction of the World Trade Centre. The sheer perfection of form of these two enormous towers, along with the name 'World Trade Centre', suggests a powerful symbol of global unity. It provides a *raison d'être*.

The moment the planes hit the towers and photographs were taken, not only the towers, but the images, became icons in themselves. Can it be said that an icon only becomes a true icon at the point when it becomes a memory and no longer exists as something solid? Is an icon a natural phenomenon? Is it public appeal? Is it something we mourn, aspire to and celebrate after it is gone, or is it simply a universal need to recognise a symbol, number, object, person or place which is unique and inspires adulation? How does it become an icon?

Metal Work by Johnny Lambe
Manchester

Chapter 9

South America

2003

February 2003

I didn't really know what I was doing, but three months later I resigned from my job and bought two tickets to travel overland from Mexico City to Rio de Janeiro. No one knew about this; it was to be our secret escape. I didn't know if it was the antimalaria drug I had been prescribed or if I was cracking up with the intensity of the relationship or if it was the fact that my reasonably comfortable life had plunged into lone chaos. Maybe I am not in love at all, but just in love with the idea of being in love. Alarm bells had begun to ring the night before we flew to Mexico City. Jason had been putting us up for the past few months. I was forced out of my previous accommodation by the homophobic fiancée of one of my dear friends from school. She was woken up at 3 a.m., after a night of red wine and marijuana, by the bang of a head being smashed against the partition wall. My friend cried and threatened not to come along. Secretly I am hoping he won't. The relationship is doomed.

The next night, as we toasted the first night of our journey, I threw back my first tequila and vomited it right up. Two hours later we found ourselves tearing lumps out of each other in a cell-like hotel room.

A few blissful weeks followed as I resigned myself to my entrapment. The irony was that I'd left England to find some sort of freedom, and in doing so had imprisoned myself.

At 1 a.m. the bus pulled into the station. I did not have enough money for a hostel—just about enough for a taxi. The plan was to go to a large Western Hotel, explain my situation and persuade them to let me stay on the promise that I'd find the cash for them the next day.

I asked the driver to take me to the Zócalo, assuming that was a safe bet. The Zócalo was deserted! I tried a couple of hotels, but received a hostile reception. Surprise, surprise. No one would trust me enough to take my battered passport. I was on the streets on my own. The police came along to explain that there was a curfew. If I did not get off the streets promptly, I'd be put in a cell for the night. PANIC!

I seemed to be attracting the attention of someone in the shadows across the street. He was my only hope, so I walked across and asked him in my pidgin Spanish if there were any hostels nearby. I listened to his warning about *los peligros* (the dangers), etc. and then followed him through the dark streets.

We knocked on the doors of countless hostels and dosshouses. Reluctantly, my 'guide' took me into the market area. He passed me a brick and picked one up for himself, presumably for our self-defence. At the end of the marketplace he banged loudly on a barred gate into what looked like a homeless shelter. A huge man in a loincloth came to the door, and after much muttering between the two men I was pulled through the gate and down a corridor into a cell.

Exhausted, I collapsed onto the makeshift bed in abject terror. I heard a car screech to a halt outside ... and then gunshots.

What seemed like hours later I heard the bolt on the door being pulled back. Too terrified to look, I buried myself and my rucksack into the dirty, sweat-soaked sheets. Someone was trying to climb into the bed with me, and I had a feeling it was the man who had opened the door to me. I could feel his sweaty stubble and smell his winey breath. A struggle ensued. I pulled the sheets tighter around me, thinking he was going to rape me. I played dead while nearly being suffocated by the sheets and the huge mountain of flesh that was smothering me.

Daylight was breaking when I surfaced. I was alone in the room, with the door barred on the outside. I had clearly been taken captive. It was 5 a.m. (Maybe they'll ask for a ransom!) The glass on the window next to the barred door was loose. Provided it hadn't been padlocked, I'd be able to push the bar across and get out into the corridor. I removed the wood from across the pane of glass, took out some of the glass and put my hand around to undo the bolt. I ran down the corridor, unlatched the front door and headed back through the market to the city centre.

It was a national holiday. I had no money and hadn't eaten for forty-eight hours. I didn't know if my friend was in the city, and the only way to find out was by checking my emails. This proved to be nigh on impossible, as I looked like a tramp and everything that was open was guarded. Even the fucking McDonald's had two guards in front, as if people wanted to steal Big Macs.

I got directions to a place about five minutes away. It was the only internet café open on the holiday.

I told my story and convinced the guy to let me check my emails. Later I found my friend at the five-star Majestic. He had been beaten up pretty badly while he was looking for me around the bus terminals.

Dreamy times at Mazuna followed: the sun sparkling on the sea, swinging in hammocks, or watching in the water as a stingray swam past.

The beautiful bodies on the beach were a distraction. The nights were spent smoking with Israelis and swimming. A filmstrip was shown one night of the beach and a mattress that had been fucked in by too many generations of backpackers.

An Argentinian came to talk to us on the platform outside our room. He told us of the horrors of Nicaragua. I'm sure he was just trying to scare us. I'd begun to feel poorly; large doses of marijuana and fear induced the sweats and a panic attack. My friend fanned me to sleep as his grandmother had done to him when as a child his mother left him under her care.

We travelled through the mountains of southern Mexico and took a boat, sailing past guerrilla camps to Guatemala.

On the River
Mexico 2003

We stopped at the island of Flores, where it rained frogs, then on to the Rio Dulce (the sweet river). There, at an orphanage, we swam naked off the jetty at night and made plans for the months ahead.

Next stop was San Pedro Sala. The constant travelling, lack of sleep, excruciating head and language difficulties had taken their toll. We were sick of the sight of each other.

The antimalaria tablets still seem to have a maddening effect. They make me feel claustrophobic, especially if I have anything to drink.

We went to a bar full of prostitutes and gays. This bar was rough as fuck. Things got hazy. We chatted to locals who took us on a rugged system tour to a gay club. We were propositioned on all sides.

The only memory I have was arriving back at the hotel covered in blood, with ripped clothing. My travellers' cheques, money and documents were ripped up. The room was trashed. I had a distinct feeling of déjà vu. I picked up whatever I could salvage and took a bus to the beach, feeling distraught. I realised I had no money and no books. My friend had it all. I must find him if I was to go on with my trip.

I hopped on the blue bird back to Sao Paulo. The room which had looked like the scene of a murder had been cleaned. At the desk, no one knew where he had gone; only that he had checked out the night before. Sweating profusely, I ran around the streets looking for him. It was an hour before dark. If I wasn't careful I'd find myself on the streets again. I decided to head for Tegucigalpa, the capital of Honduras.

From: Johnny
To: Lauren
Sent: 22 May 2003

Hi Lol,
Please send this to Mum, Dad, Cheryl and Nick, as my account was shut down and I have lost all my addresses. Thanks for your mail.

Love you,
JJ XXX

Dear Mum and Dad,

Hope all is well with you. Having a fantastic time meeting lots of people, etc. Staying on a turtle reserve on the Southern Pacific coast of Mexico, at the foot of the rainforests. It is so hot here—about forty degrees—and I am drenched with sweat all day! Drinking gallons of water and eating amazing fish and mangoes.

Have had a fun journey down here via Mexico City and Oaxaca. Mexico was incredibly hectic, and its high altitude and pollution combined with jet lag made me feel a bit queasy; but, nevertheless, I had a good time. When I got to Oaxaca City (pronounced Waa-ha-ka), a wind orchestra was playing 'Swan Lake' in the Zócalo. There was a very vibrant European feel.

The food has been amazing. I have decided to eat only street and market food, and also to cook for myself to preserve funds. The food always seems fresh, and at busy stalls I think you are less likely to get bacteria than in restaurants with poor hygiene.

My Internet time is just about over now, so I'm going to sign off. I will stay here at the beach for a couple more days, to give me some time to see the crocodiles in the mangrove swamps, before heading down to Chetumal on the Guatemala border. I should be in Lago Atitlan, Antigua, to climb some volcanoes before long. I'm hoping to sort out some relief work for Nicaragua. A film producer called Lyndsey, from New York, is going to help me sort that out, as she has spent some time there making documentaries.

I'll email again soon.

Love you,
J

From: Johnny
To: Lauren
Sent: 2 June 2003

Hello All,

Hope you are well. I'm fine and well in Rio Dulce, Guatemala—close to the border of Honduras and the Caribbean Sea. I've been having a great time. I went horse riding through the mountains in Mexico to some Indian villages, where the religion seems to be a mixture of Christianity and Voodoo and they sacrifice chickens in the churches! They also do this funny thing where they have Coca Cola blessed at the altar. They drink it and burp for ages and ages in front of the icons to get rid of their demons. I hope it works for them. Very strange indeed!

Lauren and Cheryl, you would have loved the riding. We were galloping full pelt across the mountains, cowboy style.

The weather here is so changeable, from torrential rain to freezing temperatures to forty degrees sweltering heat. It can be hard to adjust. I was ill for a few days, but just stayed in bed and am right as rain now.

I have been shooting a lot of videos, particularly of music and dancing. Tomorrow morning I am taking a small boat up the river to some sulphurous waterfalls where the birdlife is meant to be incredible and you can swim with tropical fish. Hopefully, there'll be no crocodiles this time, as I had one snap at me the other week at the turtle reserve, which gave me a bit of a fright.

I will spend tomorrow night at the small town of Livingston on the Gulf of Honduras, where there is a strong Jamaican influence, lots of reggae and jerk chicken.

Hopefully, I've got some bar work in Costa Rica in a few weeks. From there I will get a flight across Panama and Columbia to Ecuador, where the Amazon begins. Voluntary work in Managua, Nicaragua, will be between now and then. Painting an orphanage. Loads of orphans left after Hurricane Mitch in 1998.

It's the rainy season here, and I've never experienced rain like it. Thankfully, it doesn't last all day; it only comes in the evening. When it comes, you know it is raining, all right. Have met some nice Israelis and Australians, and also some funny Americans. Always good for a laugh. Drop me a line to let me know your news.

Please, Lauren, send this to Mum, Dad, Cheryl and Nick. Thanks to you and Cheryl for the mails.

Love you all loads.

Speak soon.

Ciao,
J XXX

From: Johnny Lambe
To: Lauren
Sent: 23 June 2003
Subject: *Hola Familia*

Thanks for your emails. Glad all is well. Sorry I didn't write earlier, but had to get over the stress of writing a long email to you last week and losing the whole lot.

I'm still here in León, Nicaragua, and enjoying it a lot. I've become so busy, that I can hardly find the time to think. Started training at the Academia Europa last week for a TEFL. The free training is two hours a day for two weeks, after which I can start teaching on a wage of 37 cordoba an hour—just over $2. So if I do five hours a day, I should cover my expenses. Some teachers are doing up to fifty hours per week. Too much for too little, me thinks. The teaching methods are pretty Americanised, and they expect you to give the students high fives when they do well, and all that malarkey. You have to be super enthusiastic at all times.

Apart from that, I have been having a Spanish lesson every morning with one of the university professors called Carla. That is coming along well. I will keep them going daily for the next week or so to get the fundamentals in place. It's getting to be quite expensive ($3.50 per lesson).

In the evenings, I've been working one-to-one with a few students from the language centre. They help me practise Spanish, and I help them with their grammatical problems. I have also been giving lectures on British culture and politics at the university for two hours in the evening and am directing a short play with an anti-drugs message—called *Be Yourself*—for the town fiesta, where I'll be their special guest this week!

I have moved from the hostel I was staying in to a little house with Canadian and Dutch volunteers who are building an orphanage just outside the city. The rent is $25 per month, so it makes sense. The house is pretty basic. There is a kitchen with a fridge, so I can prepare simple meals—as I did yesterday for six people. We had Spanish omelette and nice salsa, which we ate off banana leaves, for lack of plates. There is a little yard at the back of the house with a herb garden. In it there are tropical versions of oregano and basil that have leaves the size of your hand but taste just the same as they do in Europe. We also have lime, orange, mango, banana, papaya and coconut trees, with plenty of fruit on them—which is great for cooking, making drinks or just eating off the tree— AND a gaggle of chickens and ducks.

There are some nice places here called *comedores*, which are canteen-style restaurants provided for students, where you can eat enormous portions of rice, salad, meat or beans, with a nice glass of fresh melon juice, for next to nothing.

I have yet to try the local delicacy: a soup made with iguana! In the markets you can watch it being made, and I have filmed the old ladies going about their daily work of preparing these huge iguanas to make soup. Fair enough, you say, but the whole thing takes place while the creature is still alive and wriggling about in their hands. Meanwhile, the other iguanas wait in line, like lambs to the slaughter.

Method – First they cut off the head, legs and tail. Then they skin it, extract the eggs and finally chop it into chunks to put in the soup. It is only after the last stage that the iguana gives up the fight and stops thrashing around—pretty gruesome, but fascinating to watch.

Another interesting experience was last Sunday, when I went with my Dutch friends—Martina, Jores and Yohan—and some of the local Nicas (extremely nice people who are running a bar and youth hostel while the owners are away) to the rooster-fighting arena. The 'sport' is legal here, and is quite a spectacle. The winner of the fight is the cockerel that is left alive after fifteen minutes of fighting. These birds don't just peck each other to death; they have razor blades strapped to their beaks and claws, so you can imagine that there is a lot of bloodshed. The atmosphere in the crowd is electric as they gamble among themselves on the bird of their choice. I was lucky enough to get in the ring to film one of the fights.

I've got to go now, as I have a lesson shortly, but will be in touch as soon as I can. The weather is stiflingly hot—forty degrees—but it rains most of the time, and the thunder and lightning is apocalyptic.

Loads of love to you all, and a special Happy Belated Birthday to Ruari W.

J XXX

Johnny with Ruari

From: Johnny Lambe
To: Lauren
Sent: 9 July 2003 20.00
Subject: *Hola*

Hello All,

Thanks for all the emails, and sorry for not getting back to you individually; but that doesn't mean I love you any less. Things are going along pretty much the same here. Teaching English at the European Academy every weekday and Saturday, from 7–11 a.m. and 3–8 p.m., so not much time to do anything else. Had a funny experience when I did my play, *Be Yourself,* last week. One of the students who was playing the bad guy didn't turn up, so I had to stand in for him. Dressed up as a gangster, I walked across the stage, tripped over a microphone lead, forgot my lines and came out with "I've been down on the bitch with some bitches" instead of "I've been down on the *beach* with some bitches". The whole thing was a fiasco, but the audience found it very funny and we got good applause, though the principal of the *Centro de Idiomas* looked a little dismayed.

At the end of the day, I was awarded an Honorary Diploma from the University of Nicaragua for the work I've been doing for them—very kind. There was a big party afterwards, which lasted for two days, including an eight-hour concert by local band—La Rassa—who rocked!

Apart from that, not a great deal of excitement. I've met some really wicked locals and travellers. The community here is so small, that everyone knows you and knows what you've been doing. It is a bit freaky at times, when people come up to you on the street and know what you've eaten for lunch and with whom. Yesterday a few of us went to the nearby beach on the Pacific—Las Peñitas—which is absolutely beautiful.

To get around, we just hitchhiked, as everyone drives pickup trucks, so it is great to sit in the back with the wind in your hair, watching the volcanic landscape go by.

The beach has a great lagoon to swim in, and they cook the most amazing fish on the shore. Unfortunately, I got bitten four times on the arm by someone's pet monkey. They were really cute, and climbing all over me, but really didn't like it when I stopped playing with them. Luckily, they didn't break the skin. I spoke to the owner, a French lady, who said they were very healthy, so I'm not really worried about it.

As we were swimming, we could see a cyclone rip across the horizon. Once again our timing was really bad, and within five minutes of getting out of the water, the storm from hell arrived. The streets were thigh deep in water, and we were thirty kilometres away from home. Fortunately, after wading through the streets for half an hour, we got to higher ground and found someone crazy enough to drive us back through the most spectacular storm ever; all the time fearful that we would be struck at any minute by the enormous forks of lightning. All very exciting indeed.

Anyway, I'm going to go now. It was great to talk to you on Monday, Mum and Dad. I'm thinking of staying here for a couple of months, as it is good fun being a teacher, and travelling seems like such a hassle at the moment.

Speak soon,
J XX

From: j.lambe@
To: johnnylambe@
Cc: lauren@
Cc: cheryl@
Cc: nicolas@
Sent: 9 September 2003 12.56

Dearest Johnny,

It is such a relief to hear from you. I had a feeling all was not well, as I know you wouldn't leave it a whole month without contacting us. The image you painted of the other patients with dengue fever, vomiting into basins of green phlegm, reads like a horror story. So glad your friends were able to bring you fresh fruit, vegetables and some food.

I think your guardian angel was watching over you. We have been anxious and sending powerful, positive love vibes to you. I am sure you could sense these. We thank God you are on the mend and back in touch with us again.

I think San Sebastián would be a great place for you. It has good memories for us as a family; not only for Dad and me with the gang, but, of course, for Grandma Lambe, who always talked about being saved from drowning by the lifeboat. She always seemed a bit conflicted about the rescue: what was worse for her, the near drowning or the men pulling her out, causing her to lose her top and display her 'big diddies' as she called them? That did make us laugh, and, of course, Dad recounted it at the beach in San Sebastián. I think there is positive energy in San Sebastián for many reasons. Your Spanish will be very useful and you'd be able to pop along to Innisfree, only five hours away.

We are finally getting some rain, and it is a welcome relief. Please give yourself a big hug from Dad and me. We love you so very much.
xxxxxxxooooooo

17 September 2003
To: Lauren
From: Johnny Lambe
Subject: FW: 'The Longest Journey-Mao'

Hello Mum and Dad,

Everything is well. Still in León for another week until I finish working at the Academy. It has been Independence Celebrations here for three days, so everything is shut and I have been at the beach. I am having a few problems with the insurance company about getting back the money I paid for the hospital before I return to England. I need the money in order to book my flight from Panama to Lima, Peru or Ecuador, thus avoiding Columbia. There are no road connections between Central and South America, and it is far too dangerous to try by land without huge amounts of funds for bribes, etc. I hope to get something sorted in the next week.

I have planned my route by land through Peru and Bolivia, and have a couple of friends who might be joining me, which would be great. I get back to the UK on 12 November, as I will not be able to extend my ticket beyond this date. Please don't worry, as everything is fine and I feel totally back to normal.

Love you lots,
J XXXXXXXXXXX

From: j.lambe@
To: Johnny Lambe
Sent: 27 September 2003 15.02

Glad you are sorted. Spent last night with Cheryl's friend Christine's parents and her aunt and uncle who live at St Ferme in the middle of the vineyard— real big-hearted 'Yaaawwkshire' folks. Colin (her Dad) has been picking grapes. He is a larger-than-life character and her Mum is a sweetheart. Judith and Stanley are also very kind. They are all coming for dinner on Tuesday night. Talk soon and *vaya con Dios* (go with God).

Mum and Dad xxxx

From: Johnny Lambe
To: j.lambe@
Sent: 6 October 2003
Subject: Bon Voyage

Hey Mum and Dad,

All's well. Have been travelling pretty much constantly since I last emailed. Took a flight from Panama City to Quito, Ecuador, and am now in Cuenca. Ecuador is an absolutely stunning country, and the climate is cooler. It is great to be out of the furnace that was Nicaragua. I'll write later on today with full details.

Love you both lots, and good to hear you have met some nice people.

XXXXXJ

To: j.lambe@aliceadsl.fr
From: Johnny Lambe
Sent: 28 October 2003 00.38
Cc: cheryl@
Cc: lauren@
Cc: nick@
Subject: Hola Familia

Hi Everyone,

Hope you are all good and well. Thanks so much for your emails. Sorry not to get back sooner, but have been constantly travelling for the past month.

Left Nicaragua at the start of October, and it was a total relief to get out of the fiery-furnace temperatures.

Since then I've been travelling like a maniac in order to get back to Rio in time to catch the flight back to London on 11 November. Stopped briefly in San José, Costa Rica, which was very interesting, as the city is pretty modern and after Nica it felt a little like going back to the future. From there I took a bus to Panama City and had a quick look at the canal before getting a flight to Quito, Ecuador—great people, easy to travel, relaxing and stunningly beautiful scenery. Had a great time in the hot baths at Baños and hiking in the mountains. This was followed by an eight-hour ride on the roof of a train, with about half a million tourists. Amazingly, we arrived the next day in Cuenca, just in time for the second International Film Festival. Hung about at that for a couple of days, meeting a few people and watching good films. Straight on to Peru, where I ended up having to wait a few days in Máncora. The beach was nothing to write home about; it was windy and the sea was freezing cold.

From there it was thirty-six hours on the bus to Yurimaguas in Amazonia and a trip to Iquitos through rainforests on a cargo boat transporting, among other things, a herd of cows, four million bananas, a load of chickens, a few Catholic missionaries and a band of Peruvian musicians. On the second night on board it didn't seem we would make it, as we were told there was too much cargo and the boat was sinking. The message was "put on life jackets and be ready to jump".

Iquitos is absolutely incredible. Famed as the largest city in the world unapproachable by land, it feels like a great big island in the middle of the jungle. Went to the most incredible markets at Belen, which is a floating shanty town on the Amazon, with 20,000 inhabitants; and you get around by boat to all the different houses or stalls, which are either on rafts or stilts. The markets there sell everything from aphrodisiacs to endangered species: tigers, turtles, monkeys and birds of prey. It's the end of the dry season, so not floating at the moment, but it was spectacular just the same. Some of the things they eat are totally unbelievable: whole guinea pigs, turtle and tarantula. Having been laughed at by a few girls who were munching happily on them, I succumbed to eating a barbecued grub the size of my thumb, which was much tastier than you might imagine—but I didn't rush back for more.

The next day I was taken on a horticultural tour through the jungle to have a look at all the plants used in medicines. Both the bark and roots of cat's claw are used by indigenous tribes to treat, among other things, arthritis, stomach ulcers, dysentery and fevers—pretty fascinating.

On the final day in Iquitos, Jimmy, an Alsatian conservationist (the owner of the hostel that I stayed in) and his assistant, who was a rugby player from Guildford, invited a group of us to go downstream to visit his orphanage for endangered animals, provided we all chipped in for petrol.

The orphanage was like a dream come true: to play with baby tigers, jaguars, sloths and monkeys. I even held a thirty-foot anaconda and a crocodile. I had photos taken with them in which I'm sure I'm as white as a ghost, because I could feel the colour draining from my face. The day ended with a swim with pink dolphins in one of the tributaries of the Amazon.

During the trip, I met a really nice German filmmaker called Candy who had been shooting a documentary about one of the indigenous tribes who live in the village flanking the river.

On Monday I got a boat that arrived late Friday afternoon in Pucallpa. After five days of the most gruesome slop dished up into my Tupperware box, I was ready to eat my arm. I don't know exactly what gruel was, but I'm sure even Oliver Twist would not have asked for more. Apart from the food, the boat trip was a great experience. You just hung your hammock on the top deck and that was you for five days, spending time reading, writing, looking at wildlife, seeing remote settlements and meeting the other passengers, which cannot be helped, as so many people get on the boat, that the hammocks end up three tiered and about ten metres square—always room for more …

I think the five days on the boat, including food, cost about ten quid. I got off the boat and straight onto the bus for Lima. The bus trip was quite an amazing ride. I fell asleep going through dense jungle and woke up at 6 a.m. to bleak mountainous landscapes, llamas and funny little Peruvian people in indigenous costume!

Lima is a huge city. It is very dirty and smoggy, but the architecture is magnificent and it has a great Chinatown. What a relief to eat something different from the normal stodge.

Going to the bullfight was a real highlight—something I'd always wanted to do, despite the cruelty of the whole thing. The spectacle is totally amazing, like some sort of barbaric ballet. The relationship between the bull and the toreador is fascinating: intense and graceful, right up to the moment the bull dies. It's a place to be seen for upper-class Limans, and as Grampa Lambe used to say, "You can smell the money."

Despite having paid for the cheapest seats, I managed to blag my way into the best seats, telling the guards it was my dream, etc. Sitting along from me, surrounded by bodyguards, was none other than Tina Turner, who must have been taking a holiday in Lima.

In an hour's time I am getting a twenty-eight-hour bus to the Bolivian border. Despite recent problems, I have to cross the Bolivian border to get to Brazil, and it is too late and too expensive to go any other way. The British Consulate has released a statement that things are fine here now and tourism will continue as normal.

I'd best go now, as I want to have plenty to eat before getting on the bus.

Lots and lots of love to you all, and I can't wait to see you when I get back in less than two weeks.

XXXXXX J

Chapter 10

London

2003

I came back to the UK in the autumn of 2003, and was met at the airport by Mum and Dad. I was feeling tired, dirty and hungry, and was wearing a pair of long-length beige shorts, a pastel T-shirt and the sandals that had accompanied me on all my travels.

Mum's eyes wandered over me from my face to my feet, and back up to my face again, observing the long hair, pale, stubbly face, dusty sandals and dirty feet—my cool traveller look. "Oh, Johnny, you look like an angel with dirty feet," she said, wrapping me in her arms. A handshake and a quick hug from Dad. "Hello, Jonboy." Their 'boy' had returned safe and sound. Mum and Dad were so happy to see me safe, but I think Mum sensed that I had changed.

When I recovered from my journeying and was feeling rested and well fed, it was back to London—déjà vu all over again. I was lonely and missed the sunshine and open spaces. Lack of funds, no permanent home and taking whatever work came along, my life continued in its usual pattern. Any free time was spent on art work.

I was too proud to ask for help or to confide in the family. After all, I'd survived in South America all by myself, so I could do it in London.

I was still conflicted about so many things, and the lifestyle I had chosen didn't make for security. While I was at home, Mum's attempts to make me talk failed; perhaps she asked the wrong questions or didn't really want to know the answer. She'd come into my room in the morning while I was half awake. She didn't say anything; she just stood in silence looking at me lying curled up. It was as if she was trying to get inside my head to understand who I was. I was having none of it. So questions and answers remained unspoken.

Back in London, anger was the driving force I used to help overcome my loneliness and frustration. Letters and phone calls to the family became infrequent. Mum kept me up to date with family news, as did the others. She told me when things had calmed down that the mantra became "Have you heard from Johnny?".

Knowing of my strong attachment to Grandma Lambe, Mum wrote to me on 8 October 2004.

Dearest Johnny,

Just a line to tell you what is happening and to ask if you have a landline or an address where we can contact you in case of emergency. You will know from my text that Grandma has been taken into a secure home for psychiatric evaluation, as the Shore Road is considered to be an unsafe environment for her. I'm sure she hasn't been eating, and as a result she had a fall. You know how faddish she is about food: no eggs, no chicken, because of Edwina Curry. She'd often say that "you can never be too rich, nor too thin". She didn't eat very much at the best of times. Selective hearing as always, she turned a deaf ear to mad cow disease and didn't give up her little steak, but it probably became difficult to get it, as there was no longer a butcher nearby. She lost heart after Gramps went into the nursing home. Fighting with him had kept her alert and alive, and the loneliness was too much for her.

Foot and Mouth Disease 2001

Apparently, she is now sitting up talking about her son who lives in the South of France and demanding a taxi home. According to all reports, she will be kept there for a few weeks and then moved, possibly to the same place as Gramps. I've been looking at some photos of her and Gramps. She was so beautiful. It is unfortunate that she wasn't able to listen to advice, and now her avant-garde attitude is regarded as selfishness and madness. She considered herself to be a loner, but forgot that she had the love of her life to wind her up and keep her sane. Dad is very upset. He and Joe will go over soon, but it is best that she accepts she can't go home anymore. I will be sorry to leave Monségur, as this is my favourite season. Temperatures in the high twenties and pool twenty-four degrees. Fig trees growing well, especially the one you and Jason planted, but no fruit this year. Maude gave me a load of figs, so I made some amazing *confiture* (jam) which is as good as the *cerisier* (*cherry confiture*) with the *brebis* (sheep cheese). I hope you get to taste some when I get back. I have started a super French class in Miramont, but unfortunately it will have to go by the board.

I enjoyed the visit to Barcelona, but I'd never want to live in Spain, despite the beautiful beaches. I do wish you'd been able to get down on your own, but I realise it is hard out there. Have I ever told you about the butterfly and its metamorphosis from egg to larva to pupa into a butterfly? The first three stages to become a pupa take place in the safety of the cocoon. When it is time to become an adult, the final struggle begins. A little boy saw the pupa struggling to get out of the cocoon and wanted to help. He took a pair of scissors and cut the cocoon. Naturally, the pupa died, as it wasn't able to complete the transition necessary for new life. To struggle is an important part of evolution and makes us strong.

London – Butterfly on Felt by J. Lambe

Butterflies represent transience; they are like life, which is always changing, unlike the one thing in my life which will never change: my love for my elder and very special son.

I don't know if you will ever receive this letter, Johnny, but it helps me to write to you. Perhaps we can get together for a little chat *à deux* (together), either in Brighton or London. It's been a long time since we had a real talk. Don't be a stranger, and as the song says, 'Always look on the bright side of life'.

Mum and Dad xxxxx

Chapter 11

A Career Develops

2004

The turbulent times Johnny was experiencing are perhaps reflected in the venting letters to his Dad and me . He was always mercurial and there is nothing like a good vent to help people to bounce back and overcome difficulties .However positivity soon returned.

> To: j.lambe@aliceadsl.fr
> From: Johnny Lambe
> Sent: 11 October 2004
> Re: Family News
>
> Dear Mum and Dad
>
> I am in a very difficult place at the moment.
>
> I shall need to arrange for a van to come and collect my things from your house in Brighton, so would be grateful if you would let me know when you expect to be back in the country. Also, I should appreciate, if you are driving over here, that you return my paintings, which are being ruined and poorly stored at your house in France. I hope it will not be too much effort on your part, or my father's part, to let me access my things in your garage, as it seems to have caused great hardship in the past. I shall be sure to take everything to avoid any problems of this type in the future.

22 October 2004 09.31

Re: *La Famille*

Hi Mom,

I've been working at Saatchi and Saatchi a few days a week for the past fortnight, helping out on one of the creative teams, which has been quite fun, but I think this division is closing and moving elsewhere. Otherwise, all is well. Just about finished decorating my room. I will be glad to get my things back, as I think this is somewhere I will stay for quite a while. I've been teaching through an agency, and have five students altogether—all boys between the ages of ten and fifteen. My favourite pupils are the Bangladeshi brothers, Rid and Shahnur (ten and eleven), who think I am the best thing since sliced bread and can't wait to tell me their news every week when the lesson is over. It makes me feel great to know I have gained their confidence. They are coming along in leaps and bounds. I have a meeting with an art director next week who has won lots of prizes for his television commercials and is looking for an assistant. It won't be full time, but could bring in good money. Otherwise, I am enjoying freelancing, as I get to meet lots of different people and don't feel I have to get tied down to something I don't really want. I'm a little worried, as I think there is less work in the winter months because nobody wants to shoot in the limited hours of daylight.

Am desperately hoping I can sort out my driving soon, as my agent has told me this will make a considerable difference to the amount of work I get and the amount I get paid. It will also mean I'll be able to move into films on two- to three-month contracts and just do commercials as a filler. This is something I will enjoy, as I will feel I am controlling my work and not feel it is controlling me.

Sorry to hear about the grandparents, but just have to accept that some things are beyond our control, however unideal they are. I'd best get on, as I think the producer is on her way back to the office. Then it will be 'all stations'.

24 August 2005

Worked all last week directing a commercial for a company called Guerilla, and now have a month's work as production manager for a company called Coast on a series of documentaries about small businesses for HSBC. Getting paid £180 a day. The best two jobs of my life, all through determination. Perhaps I should go and sell package holidays for £5 an hour.

***

I still had many unresolved issues with Mum and Dad, so I wrote a letter to each of them, which was cathartic for me. Now I am free to get on with my life.

Mona,

1. I find your writing totally irrational and many of your arguments lacking any foundation whatsoever.
2. I have been working from 8 a.m. till 8 p.m. for the last four months in order to improve my job prospects. I think it is a very constructive use of time for someone with 'no hope'.
3. I have spent the day in the library—an action that can be seen as 'sitting on my arse' in the literal sense.
4. I most certainly was not pissed last night, and I am not always pissed. I chose to stay in Geraldine's spare bed as a convenience, and also to be near to the library.
5. I am sorry that I misjudged the efficiency of our Great British Royal Mail Service. I will not do so again in a hurry.
6. I am sorry for any inadequacies not covered by this note—but obviously to list them all would use up too much space.
7. THANK YOU BOTH VERY MUCH FOR ALL YOUR SUPPORT AND FOR GIVING ME THE OPPORTUNITY TO REACH MY GOALS—IT HAS NOT GONE UNNOTICED!

Your adoring son,

Jonathan

Dear Dad,

I can't talk to you; no one can. I wish I could like you, but I can't. Why can't you be a normal, generous human being? You will receive so much back. I know you have the capability, so please don't write yourself off as incompatible with the rest of us, as we all love you. You are so knowledgeable and have all the potential to make yourself a respectable human being, but at the moment you have just given up on life, and it makes everyone very sad. Please try, as it will make your future so much happier. I really don't know what else to say, but you know where happiness lies, and if you don't …

Think about it. You can really make yourself happy through other people.

JOHNNY

THINK ABOUT IT

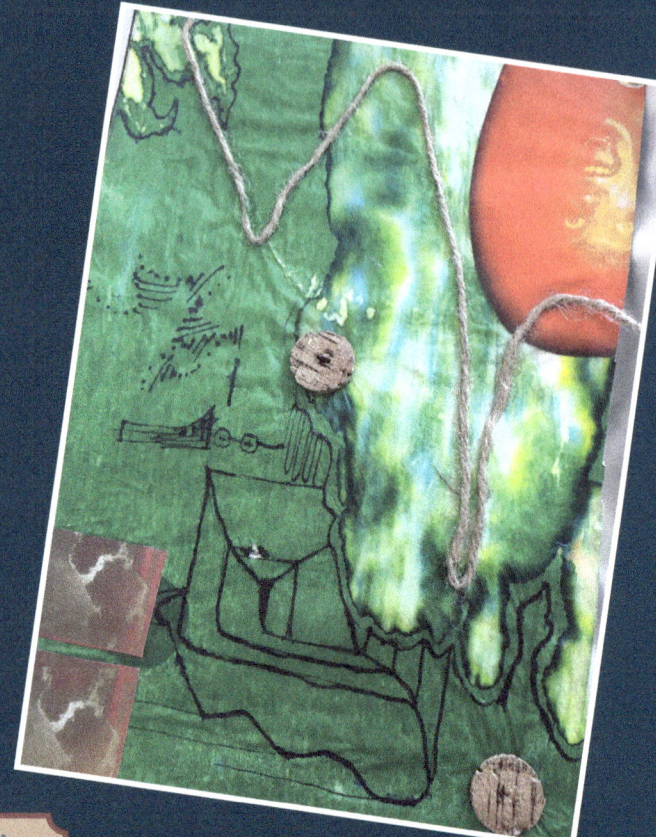

"The Joy of Colour"
by Johnny Lambe

"The Joy of Colour"
by Johnny Lambe

Chapter 12
Une Periode de Calme
(A period of calm)

I'm happiest when occupied, so the years 2006–2008 were good. I was working hard, travelling, filming, writing, doing some art work and spending time with the family.

In 2006 Nick and Arabella decided to get married, but first of all we had the stag do. It was epic. A thirty-six-foot yacht was hired to sail from Tenerife to Gran Canaria. I was designated quartermaster and happy to oblige, not taking into account that my experience of boating was limited. I enjoyed the sea, I liked boats and had never been seasick. Famous last words! Five days at sea in a small craft proved to be challenging. A vomit fest ensued, which brought to mind the pie-eating contest in *Stand by Me*. Therefore, quartermaster's provisions were limited to Haribo and beer. Nick's stag do was a great success and a crazy memory for us both, and of course the old adage, 'what goes on tour, stays on tour', applied.

The wedding took place in the beautiful little church of St Endellion, near Delabole, Cornwall—a mile from the sea and surrounded by fields. Sir John Betjeman said, "The church goes on praying, even when there is no one in it."

We stayed in a cottage on the farm. A marquee was erected for the wedding reception. Cheryl's friend Emma played the harp while we were having canapés, to the delight of all the guests. After dinner it was all-singing, all-dancing. Will, a friend of Nick's, contorted his body to take photographs at impossible angles of the dancers. The wedding day ended with Jamie M. having to be persuaded that it was not a good idea to climb to the top of the marquee. By midnight it was very dark. I walked Mum to the cottage and told her about my friend, Alexis, and the film we were working on: *Unmade Beds*.

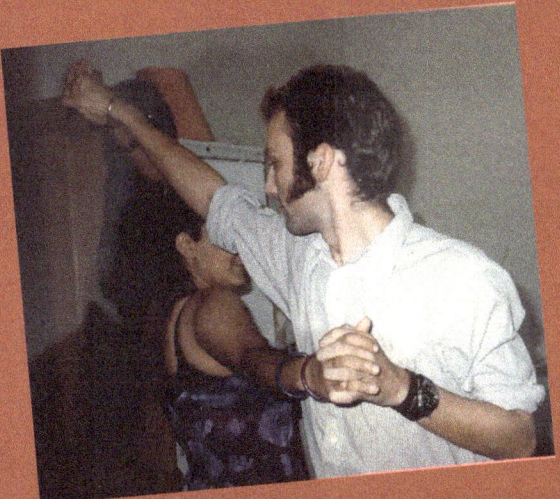

Dancing

Reading

I'm happiest when occupied

Skiing

Travelling

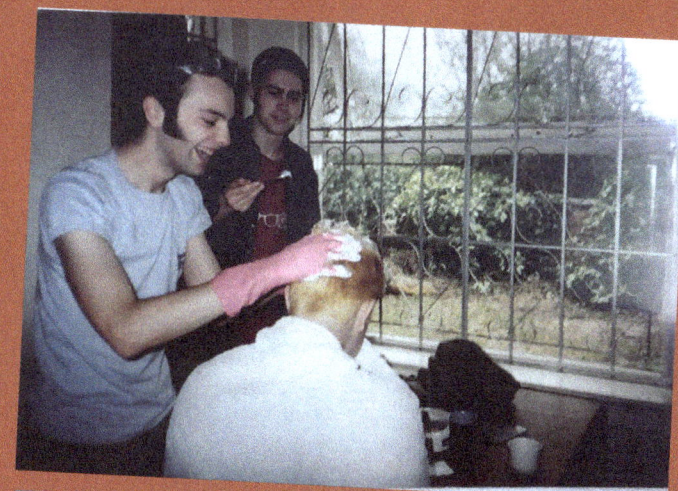

Hairdressing

Writing and Filming

Nick and Arabella's wedding

In March 2007 we had a trip to Kiruna for Lauren's wedding in the Ice Church and my thirtieth birthday. What a good time we had, driving snowmobiles over ice fields, going down the iron ore mine, learning about Sámi culture, eating amazing food with friends and chatting all the while. The wedding in the Ice Church was conducted in Swedish. Nick Johns speaks the language, but Lauren had to learn the responses. She was word perfect and managed to say *jag gör* (I do) at the appropriate moment. Well done, Lol.

I filmed the events of the day for the happy couple: Mum ironing Lauren's dress, Nicky Mora doing her makeup, walking to the church, the service in the Ice Church and drinks in the ice bar followed by dinner and dancing to the small hours.

Johnny filming Lauren on her way
to The Ice Church in Kiruna to get
married, with Mum and Dad

Johnny with Keira in Kiruna

The Johns and Lambe Families at Lauren and Nick's Wedding in Kiruna

Nick Johns, aka Big Nick, Mona and Johnny "Down the Mine" in Kiruna

Walking to Kiruna Church with Johnny 18th March 2007 Mother's Day

It is known as the Shrine of Nomadic People. We walked in quietly and sat down at the back of the church. Children were gathered around the altar singing. As we listened, we were wrapped in a blanket of calm tranquillity. When the service was over we walked down the hill to the town. I went into the supermarket to buy some pre-packed reindeer meat for Mum to take home. I gave it to her with a Mother's Day card. Usually I make a card for Mum, but I didn't have the time this year.

Mother's Day Card
by Johnny 2005

Mother's Day Card
by Johnny 2006

Mother's Day Card in Sweden 18/3/2007 from Sweden

Dear Mum,

Happy Mothers Day.

Thankyou very much for such a wonderful time here in Kiruna.

I Love you lots.

Johnny xxx

The last night of the holiday was a quiet affair, as we had an early start and two flights the next day (19 March 2007—my thirtieth birthday). We had a nice pre-birthday dinner followed by an early night.

Last night dinner in Kiruna 18/3/2007

Happy 30th, Johnny! 19th March, 2007 Johnny's Birthday. At the airport with Arabella and Nick

In July 2007 I received a very nice letter from Francis C. Wells, consultant cardiothoracic surgeon at Papworth Hospital.

> Dear Johnny,
>
> I wanted to thank you for your true professionalism and wonderful spirit of bonhomie at the live satellite transmission last week. It was a real pleasure to work with you, and I think the outcome was excellent.
>
> I hope it wasn't too traumatic for you, and I am sorry that I gave you grief with my inability to hear at the start of the operation. It was probably my otosclerosis. I wish you well for the future and hope we may work together again some time.
>
> With best wishes,
>
> Yours sincerely,
>
> Frank

I entered 2008 with optimism, looking forward to going sailing with Miss Sadie and the young recidivists from Bequia to Venezuela.

Poster by Sadie Kaye of Sailing Miss Sadie

On 19 March 2008 I came to Hove to have my birthday dinner with Mum and Dad, Lauren and Nick Johns, and a couple of friends. Mum cooked my favourite roast beef and béarnaise sauce followed by chocolate cake. It was one big piece of beef. Someone said, "I've never seen a roast that big." We didn't eat it all, and as always Mum sent me back to London with enough beef and chocolate cake to last three days.

At one point I went out to get some cigarettes. There was a lot of noise going on, so no one could hear me knocking on the door to get back in. Dad's new Mercedes was parked under the veranda, so I decided to climb onto the roof of the car. Patrick, the neighbour, came out as I was about to climb over the railing. "What are you doing there? Hey, Mona, John; there is someone on the roof of your car." The patio door opened, and Mum said, "It's all right, Patrick. It's our son, Johnny."

When the others had gone, Mum, Dad and I had a grown-up talk. Dad held my hand and Mum sat in front of us. I showed them a tiny photo of Marta which fits into the palm of my hand. Mum said, "She is beautiful, like a little Madonna."

It was back to London the next day to prepare for a flight to the Caribbean with Sadie and the boys.

***

In 2006 Nick and Arabella decided to go to work in Hong Kong. We had a fancy dress farewell party for them in Brighton in June. That was to be my last night with my brother.

Nick's going away party

Brothers in Arms

Spain Playa Daro

Camping in Zaruth Spain

***

On Saturday, 28 June, I went to Cheryl and Stu for a birthday lunch for Mum. This was the only day which suited us all. Everyone helped with the preparations for lunch, and as always, we ate too many nibbles and drank too much red wine with the roast beef and Yorkshire puddings. We went for the now-obligatory post-lunch walk along the River Adur. Little Finn walked along with me, and I recorded him singing Johnny Cash's 'Ring of Fire', which we always sang at family celebrations (Dad being a country music fan and Mum considering 'Ring of Fire' as a mantra for life). We stopped at the Old Railway for a beer, and afterwards we walked home ready for dessert—sticky toffee pudding—all blissfully unaware that this glorious day was to be our last.

Last Day With The Family 28/6/2008

I took the last train back to London and started, again, to write *My Book*. I was going to a documentary film-maker's course in Oxford at the end of July. I rang Mum on Tuesday, 22 July, before I left, to tell her I had booked a flight to Bordeaux on 1 August. I enjoyed listening to Mum's Irish lilt as she brought me up to speed on family news. Mum was excited about my visit and, of course, she would go out for a 'wee shop-up' to Marmande. The fridge would groan with supplies.

On Friday, 26 July, she did just that. On the way back home, she and Dad stopped in a little village called Lévignac for the Marché Nocturne. It was kicking, as always, with music, good street food, dancing, and friendly people. Mum and Dad decided to play 'spot the lookee-likee', and would you believe who they saw with his long white beard? 'The Butcher of Bosnia', Radovan Karadžić.

"Oh my God!" said Mum. "Surely he can't have escaped again." Karadžić was in the news at that time, as he had been captured on 21 July 2008, after thirteen years on the run. The white-bearded, man joined their table, and he and Dad discovered that they were Robert Service fans. Dad and 'Lookee-Likee' took it in turns to recite *The Shooting of Dan McGrew* and *The Cremation of Sam McGee*. Everyone was pretty merry by the end of the evening. The 'olds' were on their way to the car when they were stopped by a friend, Arthur. "It's the beautiful Mrs Lambe," he said. "How about a dance?" A perfect end to a perfect day for Mum.

Chapter 13

The End Of Our World

On Saturday morning, 26 July, Mum was in good form: happy and excited. Dad walked to the village while Mum baked some soda bread to make him bacon sandwiches. At 10 a.m. Mum suddenly felt a bit dizzy and swayed back from the hob. What is this, she thought. I have no reason to have a panic attack.

The telephone rang as Dad walked through the front door at about 11 a.m. Poor Mum and Dad. Their world was about to change forever. Mum answered, and a voice said, "Is that Mrs Lambe? This is the police. Your son, Johnny … " At this point Mum said, "John, John" and handed the phone to him.

Hearing Dad say "Yes, yes, a roof", she ran screaming into the garden. Hearing her, the neighbours came over to the hedge.

"*Mona! Mona! Que s'est-t-il passé*—What happened?"

"*Mon fils, mon fils, mon fils*—My son, my son, my son. *Il est tombé d'un toit*—he fell from a roof." The first words Mum spoke after the news of my accident were in French.

Dad made a call to Angela and David. They were with Mum and Dad in thirty minutes. Michel and Maude rang Bergerac Airport and got the last two seats on the 3.30 p.m. flight into Gatwick. At some point Dr Gerlinde Mandersloot rang from the intensive care unit at the Royal London Hospital to ask if Mum and Dad were coming. Mum replied, "If I had a private plane, I'd be there already. If Johnny understands anything, please ask him to wait for me."

It was as if an angel was opening doors for Mum and Dad. The flight was on time. They ran straight through the airport onto a waiting train, got off it at London Bridge, walked through the unmanned gates and there was a taxi waiting for a fare. The taxi took them to the Royal London Hospital. Seeing Mum and Dad's distress, he said, "Have you a problem?"

"Yes. Our son has had an accident. He is in the neurological unit."

When the taxi stopped at the hospital, Dad took out the money to pay the fare. "Not at all. This one's on me." A random act of kindness by a cabbie sent from above. Thank you.

Cheryl, Stu, Lauren, Nick, Alexis and Valentina were in the waiting room. Struck dumb is the only way to describe how they were feeling. The neurology consultant came to explain in simple terms my condition. "The stem, which is the source of life, is severed. Do you understand? Is there anyone else to come?"

"Yes! Nick and Arabella are on the way from Hong Kong. They will be here at 8 a.m. tomorrow morning."

"Very well. We'll look after Johnny until they arrive. In the morning we will do some tests for vital signs so you can see that we have done our very best for Johnny."

Mum and Dad came to the ward to see me. Standing at the head of my bed, Mum said, "Oh, Johnny. This is something I can do nothing about." She whispered a little childhood prayer:

> Now I lay me down to sleep,
>
> I pray the Lord my soul to keep.
>
> If I should die before I wake,
>
> I pray the Lord my soul to take.
>
> If I should live for other days,
>
> I pray the Lord to guide my ways.

The hospital provided a bedroom for the night. Mum was unable to rest, so she spent most of the night sitting with my right hand pressed to her cheek. A nurse came to wash me and said to Mum, "There are two boys on this ward, with two different outcomes. One will live and be a paraplegic for life; the other is Johnny."

A second nurse came by and said, "Do you think Johnny would like a palm print?"

"Yes, he would like that," Mum replied.

During the night, Hareth arrived. He'd been at a wedding in the North of England when he'd heard about my accident. He'd immediately got a train back to London to be with me. Kate Boyd Brent also came to visit with her little baby. Good friends from university.

At 8 a.m. Nick and Arabella arrive from Hong Kong.

A nurse came to the waiting room where they were gathered and escorted Dad, Mum and Nick to the ward where two specialists were by my side.

"We want you to be reassured that we have done everything we can for Johnny."

Mum was standing at the end of the bed, between Dad and Nick. She whispered to them, "Please don't let me fall."

I think at this point my spirit left my body. I wanted to film the most significant experience of my life. I perched my camera on Mum's right shoulder, and looking through the lens I saw what Mum was seeing: the consultants doing the tests for vital signs. When the first test was completed they looked at Mum and shook their heads. "No signs of life." A second test, then a third and final test. A shake of the head by the doctors, and in unison with them, Mum said, "No signs of life."

She slumped down like a rag doll, and was dragged to the waiting room by Dad and Nick. As promised, they didn't let her fall.

In the waiting room a nurse arrived to talk about organ donation. Mum was appalled at first, but she asked each of us for an opinion. We all said yes, and Hareth added, "I think Johnny would like that." The decision was made for me to be an organ donor.

Leaving me in good hands, the family drove back to Cheryl's house. Little Finn was playing with his Lego on the floor. "I like Uncle Johnny. He plays Lego with me. I don't want him to be dead."

Stu had made a delicious cassoulet for Mum and Dad. They decided to take it home to have for dinner. Mona (Mum's friend) and Bill Smith came over to lend their support and enjoy the cassoulet.

So, on the 27 July 2008 I started zooming. Way ahead of my time.

Johnny's Palm Print

Chapter 14
All Saints Church

The last week in July was hell. I wanted to be close, to watch over the gang. I could see Mum and Dad: stoic during the day, but wrapped together in anguished tears at night as they tried to drown out the noise of their grief.

Angela and David had arrived with a boot load of food. Angela took control of the kitchen, and she and David were sleeping downstairs. Uncle Edmund had come over from Ireland and was in the bedroom next door. The Mews House has paper-thin walls; every sound can be heard. A tortuous week for all ensued.

All Saints Church in Patcham was chosen for the celebration of my life. This is a Grade II listed building with Norman internal features and a thirteenth-century interior. It sits on a hilltop and has been a place of worship for 1,000 years. Mum had told me about this church after she'd been to her friend Betty's funeral there. She'd said, "We must go to look at it next time you are down." I think she had something different in mind for our visit.

Alexis and Hareth organised the music. Trish designed the cover of the *Book of Memories*. The Ginger Pig in Hove was chosen for the reception after the cremation, and Ben and Pamela very generously donated the food. Cheryl chose the flowers: the biggest sunflowers I have ever seen. Lauren's friends at Killer Creative printed out the order of service, and Lauren typed up Nick's oration. Nick brought Mum and Dad to see me at the undertakers.

All dazed with shock and grief, Mum kissed my cheek and said, "My beautiful boy."

1 August 2008

Instead of being my arrival in France, it was a celebration of my life. A truly multicultural day, with people from Spain, Italy, Ireland, Australia, Argentina, Sweden, France, England, Scotland and Wales. A drab morning in Patcham, the only bright spot was Hareth's yellow shirt which seemed to symbolise the future, rebirth and springtime. At least 200 people attended—standing room only. I was hoisted on high by Dad, Nick, Stu and Nick Johns and carried into the church. Mum walked alone behind the coffin, followed by Cheryl, Lauren and Arabella.

Lauren, my astral twin, was in the middle, so that the girls could stop her from falling. The girls looked beautiful in their black dresses with magnificent splashes of pink flowers.

Strains of music by the Pixies, Bright Eyes, Neutral Milk Hotel, The Libertines and Peter Sarstedt could be heard playing softly in the background, thanks to Alexis and Hareth.

Nick's eulogy, set the ball rolling:

> "Thank you all for being here today. It means a lot to see so many of Johnny's friends, colleagues and loved ones. Johnny does not want this to be a sombre day, as he avoided miserable situations like the plague. A wedding, a birthday or a party with free-flowing champagne is definitely more Johnny's style.
>
> "Johnny's had such *joie de vivre*—a bit of a wild child with a deep passion for the beautiful things in life, be that paintings, antiques, different cultures, film-making, music or food. At Christmas Cheryl, Lauren and I knew by the shape of our gifts that he would be sharing his passion for food again! Johnny's latest cookery book or gadget was there under the tree for each of us on Christmas morning.
>
> "Johnny chose his path in life—and *his* path only. He would often tell me that he could never work in a regular nine-to-five job and that I was mad to do it. Johnny was determined to make it as a documentary film-maker, and it was this passion that was getting him to where he wanted to be.
>
> "When we were kids, we naturally fought, as brothers do, but as we grew up we learnt to appreciate and rely on each other. We were different, but we loved each other very much.
>
> "On family holidays we spent our days trying, and most of the time succeeding, to get up to no good. Once in Figueres, northern Spain, after a day at the Dali Museum, we managed to siphon some money out of Grandma and Grampa. We headed off to buy as much peach schnapps as we could—our standard adolescent drink. We then

> trundled off to the beach, as that was the only place where we could drink it. I have a vague recollection of running away from the *Guardia Civil*. We 'evaded capture', but woke up rather unhappy parents when we got back home. Next morning we were both very hung over and refused to get out of bed. We had no choice, as we were starting the journey home.
>
> "The twists and turns through the Pyrenees, from Roses to Cerbère, en route to Collioure, was memorable to say the least. Johnny twigged that I was on the verge of being sick. He hastened this along by eating peaches and offering me a bite every five seconds. Peaches, no thank you; never again, in solid or liquid form.
>
> "I eventually succumbed to the inevitable. We pulled over to the side of the mountain for a 'sick stop', which Johnny found hilarious. Grandma Lambe was not happy, having been terrified all the way around the mountains. She said to Dad, 'I'll never speak to you again after bringing me on this bloody awful trip. I think you are trying to kill me.'
>
> "A friend who lost his brother in tragic circumstances five years ago told me this week that every day of his life he gains a little strength from the life and character of his brother. I'd like to think that we could all gain a little extra passion, determination and *joie de vivre* from the way Johnny lived his life. This would mean his loss is not in vain. I hope to hear many stories, much laughter and lots of singing later in the Ginger Pig."

Nick's eulogy was followed by Dad's reading of *The Lake Isle of Innisfree* by William Butler Yeats. After The reading of W.B. Yeats by John came Hareth and Jason. Hareth was resplendent in his sunflower coloured shirt. He talked about dance moves and university days. Jason then recalled school days at Brighton College and interrailing. The congregation sang 'One More Step Along the World I Go'. I really like the sentiments expressed in this song, especially 'And it's from the old I travel to the new; keep me travelling along with you' and 'All the new things that I see, you'll be looking at along with me'. These words make me think of zooming, and bring to mind some words Maude wrote in the *Book of Memories*: 'Johnny, *le grand voyageur*—the great traveller—*maintenant, il voyage dans l'univers*—now he travels in the universe.'

Mum's tribute was next. Grit determination and I think me whispering "You're the director, Mum" got her through this. Only at the end did she falter, but Nick was there to help her back to her seat.

Cheryl, Lauren and Ruari did a reading from *The Twits* by Roald Dahl, and Hareth, in his wonderful flamboyant manner, recalled university days. Arabella, supported by Stu, read from *Revelations 21*, verses 1–7: 'Now I saw a new heaven and a new earth, for the first earth had passed away.'

"Words of encouragement", to help us sing the last refrain.

Finally, 'Thine, be the glory, risen conquering Son'. Music composed by George Frederic Handel, and words written by Edmund Louis Budry and translated into English by Richard Birch Hoyle.

We left the church, and the background music played again while those who wished to signed the *Book of Memories*. Thanks to Trish for the inside cover.

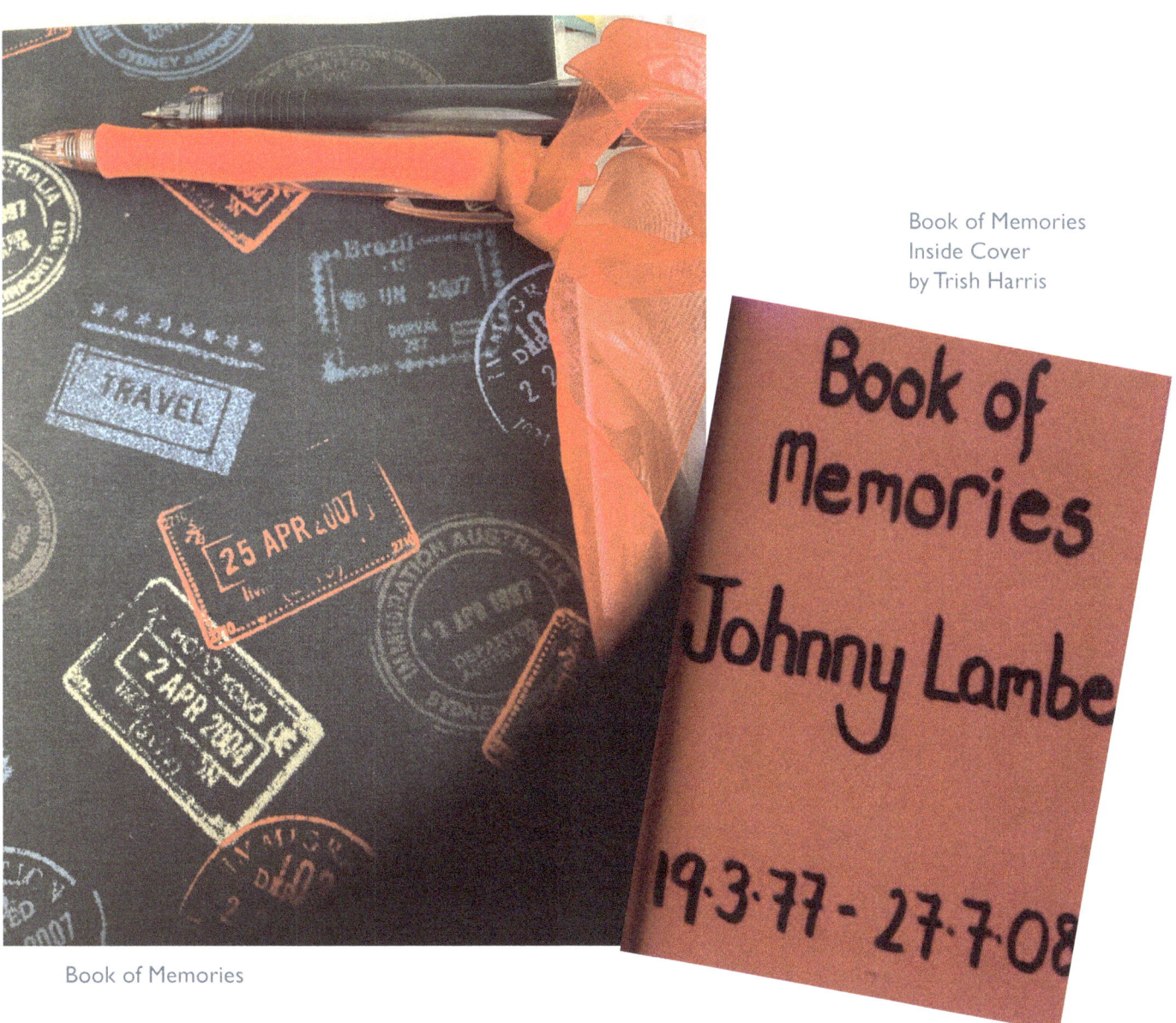

Book of Memories

Book of Memories
Inside Cover
by Trish Harris

Johnny and Marta

South Chapel, Woodvale Crematorium. A short, unendurably painful service. Wails of desolation, Mum and Dad mouthing the words of *'Non, Je ne regrette rien'*, sung by Edith Piaf, as I floated off.

The service was over, and the mood music changed, by Cyndi Lauper singing *'The Goonies 'R' Good Enough'*.

Next stop, The Ginger Pig for food, drinks and chats. A wall of sound with intermittent shouts of "Johnny", as my young friends downed shots and jumped up to toast.

Mum talked to Geoffrey and swayed to Bob Dylan's 'One Love'. She touched his face as they danced and said, "What beautiful skin."

Sadie was distraught. Mum held her in her arms to comfort her. My lovely Kate Vines came to speak to Mum, so sad and dignified, having left her father's hospital bed. Early in the evening, after a long day, Mum found a quiet table and asked for soup. A waitress brought it to her with bread and cheese.

Some friends came to say hello or goodbye. Bill Smith said, "You've given a new meaning to funerals, Mona." Another voice said, "It's me, Mona. Mark." Mum could only remember the nickname of this incredibly clever friend of Nick's. "Oh, Dopey. Thank you for coming."

Finally, Marta, the little Madonna, came—a timid little thing. "Hello, Mona. It's me: Marta. I loved Johnny so much." Dad joined them, and they sat, heads together, chatting.

It was a balmy summer night. We walked home through Hove: people in bars, restaurants, street music—a beautiful night for a stroll. Life was going on just as it should, because *Life is Beautiful* (my favourite film). Home and oblivion for Mum and Dad.

Love you both very much,

Johnny xxxxx

Images from Order of Service Celebrating Johnny's Life

Book of Memories

On 2 August Mum, Dad, Angela and David went for a drive to The Seven Sisters Country Park. I'd had fun camping there with my school friends.

A Sussex shepherd's hut and a view through some hedges dappled with sunbeams, which was like a Jackson Pollock canvas, were some of the signs which told them that "this is the place you are looking for".

The Duffs went home to Lincolnshire, Nick was in a hurry to get back to his new job in Hong Kong and Cheryl was in Brittany.

A week later they came back: Lauren, Nick, AB, Nick Johns, Dad and Mum. Around a tree they scattered my ashes and placed some flowers, then holding hands they encircled it and said, "Peace be with you."

Some passing children stopped to ask what was happening. Mum gently explained. "This is our way of remembering a young boy who died in a tragic accident."

Nearby were some 'teepees', probably made by Scouts, from branches of fallen trees. We huddled inside one, and Mum read some verses from *The Changeling* by Charlotte Mews. It seemed appropriate, as Angela had said "Johnny was a little changeling." Also, Mona, Mum's Swedish friend, had recommended it. Especially poignant were the following words:

> I shall grow up, but never grow old,
>
> I shall always, always be very cold,
>
> I shall never come back again!

I think Mum wanted everyone to realise that a different journey had begun.

John scattering flowers from friends

Mona reading 'The Changeling' by Charlotte Mews

'Victory for Johnny' photograph by Nick Johns

We set off to a nearby pub overlooking the meanders of the Cuckmere Haven.

The grey day reflected our mood, I expect.

We wanted to sit outside to enjoy the view, and we needed some head space. The waitress reluctantly showed us to a table. The overhead canopy was filled with water. A chance for a bit of mischief, me thinks. Lauren put her hand up to empty the canopy. There was a gust of wind and we all jumped back laughing as we were showered with water. "Mister Johnny, up to no good again," said Lauren.

This is a special place for me. I painted a watercolour on hessian of Cuckmere Haven as a wedding present for Cheryl.

Water Colour on Hessian
Cheryl's Wedding present by Johnny

Life returns pretty much to normal. I zoom nearby to help and be present when I can. With each passing day, more letters come through the letterbox. Dad opens the letters, Mum reads and Dad listens, becomes the daily ritual. They are feeling so very sad, but proud to read good things about *moi*, as Miss Piggy used to say.

I would like to share some excerpts from these letters with you.

North Thames Regional Transplant Coordinators

Dear John, Mona and Family,

As promised, I write now with a little information about the outcome of Jonathan's donation. Two successful kidney transplants have occurred. The recipients are a 58-year-old gentleman who had renal failure as a result of his diabetes—his new kidney is already working normally—and a twenty-nine-year-old lady who is engaged to be married. I imagine she is delighted at the new future ahead for her.

Jonathan's liver has also been transplanted into a forty-nine-year-old man. His new liver is slowly showing signs of returning to normal function.

I hope in time you are able to draw comfort knowing the difference you have made to these patients and their families. On their behalf, I thank you.

With kindest regards,

Teressa Tymkewycz

Dear Mr and Mrs Lambe,

I am sorry that I did not get a chance to meet you after Sadie's film. I think this film really portrayed our work with young people.

I am so sad to hear about your wonderful son, and we are grateful for your kind donation.

Although we never recover from the loss of a child, I hope it is of some comfort to know how he helped to change young people's lives. Please accept our deepest sympathy.

Kind regards,

The Princes Trust

Time to lighten the tone. This letter from Kim helped me when I was feeling homesick.

Magdalene College
Cambridge
17 January 1990 13.00

Dearest Johnny,

Thanks for the letter. My last exam is in an hour, so having just received your letter I decided to write a little bit now. I am also missing home. It's tough. I try to think how great it will be when I do go home. It is better to be cheerful, so SMILE!

Let's see … My birthday first. It was a bit quiet. I got, among other things, a pair of freaky slipper socks and a picture of Brighton Seafront from Cheryl. NO BOGLINS? I am very upset!

What's this about kicking one of the rugby boys in the face? Did you knock out any teeth?

It's great you are learning the violin. My teacher sounds very much like yours—YUK.

As for Flossy, she tasted lovely with roast potatoes, Yorkshire puddings, brussel sprouts and gravy! No, actually I haven't seen Flossy yet. I'll send your love to her, and I might send you a bit. Would you like that? Which part do you want? (No head I am afraid). I'll be back late. Byeeee

I'm back. By the way, I've squirted everyone here with your water-squirter. They all want to know where I got it. I just say, "It was a gift from a very special friend with a dry sense of humour." So ,you are famous here. It's time for dinner now, so I'll say *adieu*.

Love,

Kim (PTO)

PS I thought I'd change colour.

PPS Why did you have so many PS's?

Sailing Miss Sadie

My faithful one-man camera crew, Johnny and I set out to sail across the most dangerous stretch of the Caribbean Sea with a group of young recidivists.

Prior to this trip, he'd filmed an autopsy for Channel 4, which he'd considered his worst ever work experience.

Johnny has a friend who is going to get us into one of Venezuela's most notorious prisons, El Rodeo, Caracas.

The boys are getting too comfortable crewing a yacht in the Caribbean. It is time for a reality check and an altogether more urban experience. Venezuela's dirty, pulsating capital seems as good a place as any to start.

Meeting Johnny once was enough to be tickled by his amazing qualities and spirit. Those of us who were lucky enough to be loved by him in whatever way are blessed indeed.

Sometimes I sit on my balcony and weep for the loss I still feel; more often I chat to him. I can feel his presence, his love and his entertained amusement. I can hear his raucous, honest laugh as clearly as if it was yesterday.

Most of my memories of Johnny are of collapsing with laughter at something either of us did or said. Laughing at himself, laughing at, and laughing with, me.

We could crack each other up in a magical way that is rare to find. I have struggled to find anyone to make me laugh like Johnny did.

Thank you, Sadie. We had a ball.

Poster for Sailing Miss Sadie Premiere

Johnny and Hareth Uni Friends Forever

Hareth has been an amazing friend since university. I do like these texts he sent to Mum in 2005.

> Hi Mona,
> Thank you for your lovely message. It made me laugh and cry about equal measures. I had another nice one from Lauren and the juniors today. I'm currently on a bus from … to … where my mam and dad live. I've got a big bag of gear, including climbing boots and a tent, as on Boxing Day I am going surfing, trekking, climbing and camping in Portugal. The backpack is actually Johnny's: the one he took to South America. We swapped bags before I went to Sri Lanka, as Johnny's was bigger than mine. I really love it (Johnny's bag); whenever I am carrying it, which is often, he is with me. It's got a big yellow stain down the side where a tin of Peruvian was spilled over it when he was on a bus.

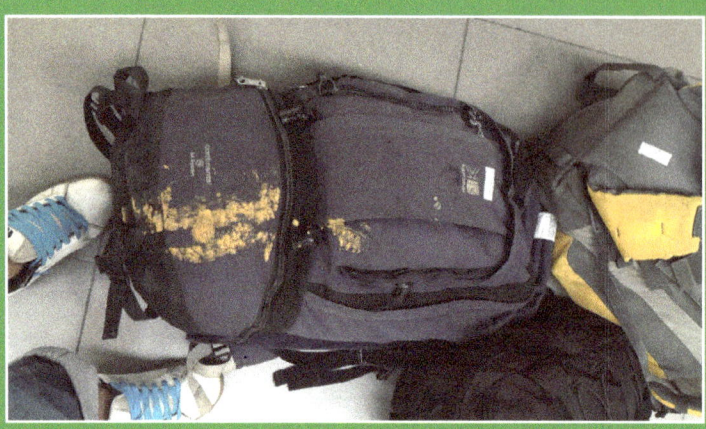

Johnny's Rucksack

A few weeks ago, due to a combination of oversized hand luggage and sentimentality, I paid a taxi driver to take this old, yellow-stained and completely empty rucksack from Stansted to my house while I boarded the plane for Barcelona. Have a nice Christmas, and I'm looking forward to seeing you in 2015.

Reply on 24 December 2015:

You are a treasure Hareth. You have painted beautiful pictures for me.

Reply on 24 December 2015:

Happy to be of service. This bag has two, maybe three, *subjects*, not *owners*, for no one owns the bag. It is a free spirit; if anything, the bag owns us. It has crossed at least four continents, witnessed all kinds of human interaction, carried objects such as llama-wool socks, alpine goats' cheese, and a Haitian voodoo dagger. Yes! This bag has many tales to tell. Perhaps it might write them down one day. x

Reply:

Do it, Hareth. You have as yet unplumbed depths. A privilege to know you. Happy Turkey. xx

Hey Lolly,

I really like your painting. Quite the cyclist, aren't I? Off to buy a baguette and some cheese in the village.

'Johnny Cycling to the Village' watercolour by Lauren Johns

It's Johnny by Lauren Johns (2008)

When I feel the wind upon my skin,
It's Johnny.

When the sun is burning bold and bright,
When I savour heavenly flavours and sip fine wine,
It's Johnny.

Every new sight and sound and wonder,
It's Johnny.
When I hear laughter and screams of delight,
When there is silence and when all is still,
It's Johnny.

When snowflakes fall and Toto rages,
Every day and all around, and when I dance and sing out loud,
It's Johnny.

When white horses race and seagulls cry,
When sunflowers sway and corn stands proud,
Every challenge and adventure braved,
It's Johnny.

When I'm in despair then courage comes,
When pain engulfs and I find a way,
It's Johnny.

When memories are pure and happiness flows,
Every hope, wish and dream comes true,
Always
It's Johnny.

'Johnny' A Poem by Lauren Johns

Water Colour by Lauren Johns for *Yintin Tales* by Mona Lambe

Water Colour by Lauren Johns for *Yintin Tales* by Mona Lambe

Great poem, sis. Love you, and thanks for the paintings you did for *Yintin Tales*. I really wanted to edit those for Mum. Now a very special letter that Kate wrote to Mum.

> Dear Mona,
>
> … This is a very difficult letter for me to write, as it is a final admission that Johnny has gone … I guess I still imagine he is off having more adventures and getting into scrapes in the way he always did. I think your comment about him being up on the broomstick with his granny was perfect. Each time I look up at the night sky, I imagine him whizzing about like Harry Potter …
>
> He had a massive impact on my life, as he did on so many others'. Your son was a man who was full of enthusiasm, with such a love of fun, laughter and life, that his company was infectious. I do miss him terribly.
>
> He literally bewitched me when I first met him. I was just nineteen. He was 'Johnny with the Hat'—way too cool for school. He is the most beautiful man I've ever seen, I thought. I could barely speak, and used to turn red when he came into the room. I did not know how anyone so enigmatic and confident would ever be interested in me … Luckily, he was, and that year was the beginning of a friendship I will cherish forever.
>
> The funny thing about Johnny was that he was such a complex character: one minute the centre of attention—pouring the drinks, cooking the food, hosting the party—and the next minute he'd be retreating to his room, listening to Classic FM (he loved the film classics show on Sunday afternoon), reading books and dreaming about going to the Slade.
>
> I hope one day I'll get to tell you about all the brilliant times I had with Johnny, from running away to Ireland and ending up in Glasgow to dancing on a float at the Notting Hill Carnival to quiet moments walking on the hills at Edale, near Manchester. Handing out our CVs in London; getting drunk in Mayfair; skiing in the Alps; staying up all night to watch the sun come up; trying to write a novel together; swimming in the sea in Brighton with a hangover; watching *Four Weddings and a Funeral* five times; painting the bathroom in my flat, and each other. So many happy

> memories of my time with him ... moments I will cherish forever. Truly, he was my first love, and now I realise how much we are a product of the people we meet.
>
> Johnny was extremely loyal to his true friends, and I know many people were affected by his death, particularly the Albion Road crew from Manchester: Neil Paul, Steven, Vern, Jaimy, Marcella, Bertie, Alex, Ed, Hareth; the list is endless.
>
> I include a book Johnny used to read to me in more reflective moments. *Jonathan Livingston Seagull* by Richard Bach. I read it again recently, and I think it sums him up quite well.
>
> Johnny never was one to mope around with a hangover. It was always onwards and upwards to better times, and always on a full stomach, thanks to his culinary brilliance.
>
> It was good to see you and John again. It reminded me of just why Johnny was like he was. On the one hand, he was much like you—life and soul, warm and bubbly, the instigator of lots of fun—but he had a lot of John in him too—considered, thoughtful and just a little shy. This is why he had so many loyal friends; he was good for the good times and good for the bad times.
>
> Take care, Mona.
> With lots of love to you and the family.
> Kate xxxxxx

Thank you, Kate, for sharing all these happy memories of when we were young and in love. I know it means a lot to Mum and Dad. BTW I enjoyed the Manchester crew Zoom call on 27 July 2020, the high point of the ghastly year of the COVID-19.

Mum got this message from Bertie (or Tiger Balm as I called her, as she always gave me Tiger Balm when I was a bit poorly).

> **From Bertie:**
> We were on the west coast of Ireland. Johnny and I went beachcombing for hours and hours. The others sent out a search party. It was one of the loveliest times I ever spent, just picking up crap with Johnny on an Irish beach. Brought tears to me today.
> Bertie (aka Tiger Balm)

Yes, it was a great day, Bertie, and I love your photographs. My yellow oilskins still get lots of wet-day outings with Lauren and the boys.

Johnny Beachcombing with Bertie
Photo by Bertie Jenkins AKA Tiger Balm

Johnny 'Gone Fishing' in West Of Ireland
by Bertie AKA Tiger Balm

Hi Al,

It was good of you and Valentina to come to visit Mum and Dad in Hove. What a nice day you had! I enjoyed seeing you make wheaten bread, with Lauren and Mum looking on, giving advice. The butternut squash soup went down a treat with the Berticot Blanc.

John and Mona on 'A Day out in Sussex with Alexis'

So glad you walked up through the forest and climbed over the wall until the landscape opened up to the amazing views over Cuckmere Haven. I know this perspective of the landscape interests you, as we have walked the path down the river.

Helping you with the translation of *Glue* and being with you at the premieres in Rotterdam, San Sebastian and London was a privilege.

The telephone call as you were leaving for the station, after your day with Mum and Dad, telling you that *Unmade Beds* is going to Sundance was the perfect end to your wonderful day. Congratulations, Al. What a talent you are! I'm looking forward to the screening on 15 December. My one-liner does makes me laugh: What will the Russian boy have for breakfast?

Unmade Beds by Alexis Dos Santos

Johnny's Bedroom with an Unmade Bed

To continue with my writing, everyone! The following is a story about 'Budgie Man'. I do hope you enjoy it.

Budgie Man

Budgie Man intrigued me because he brought back memories of a day out in London with our French friends, the Hodeberts. We walked through St James's Park, and I stood on the bridge, arm stretched out, to feed the birds at Birdcage Walk.

Johnny "Feed the Birds"

Letter of Intent – Budgie Man 1 x 23 minutes

The first time I witnessed the phenomenon that is Budgie Man was when I stumbled upon his performance in 2001. Since then, anyone I have mentioned this surreal experience to has dismissed it as a figment of my imagination or enquired as to what drugs I was taking at the time. This led me to a situation in which I have never been able to convince anyone of his existence or find anyone else who has witnessed Budgie Man for themselves.

I almost convinced myself that I was just crazy and had dreamt up this bizarre character. I banished all notions of Budgie Man to some dark corner of my mind … That is until recently, when I heard about this scheme and decided that if Budgie Man did exist after all, and if I'm not crazy, with a bit of research and a lot of luck I could have my chance to prove my sceptics wrong and reclaim my sanity in a blaze of budgie-yellow glory.

It did not take me long to track him down. So there I was, sitting beside him in the front seat of a four-wheel drive, listening to the pumping sounds of the new techno mix of his signature tune, 'I am the Budgie Man'. Budgie Man and I had an immediate rapport.

I had a surreal and highly memorable five-hour whirlwind tour of Don's favourite East End haunts. He entertained me with a constant flow of anecdotes, opinions and renditions of his songs and questionable stand-up comedy.

A documentary film about this relatively unsung hero who had been bringing smiles to the faces of Londoners for the best part of half a century would be for him a dream come true. Now I had to condense the rich tapestry of his life to a mere twenty-three-minute film.

I decided to use his songs as a device to drive the documentary and highlight various aspects of his life.

He is a charismatic, interesting and quirky individual: an ideal subject for a London documentary. He is a salt-of-the-earth gem, back from the dead three times and once dubbed 'King of the Buskers', with a side-show of twenty all-singing, all-dancing fluorescently coloured budgerigars.

I shall bring my personal perspective as a documentary film maker onto the screen and reveal in a compassionate manner the tragic events of his early years by delving below the surface of the colourful face of this performer. It will enable me to hone my ocular skills and demonstrate elements of my quirky, ironic sense of humour through the sheer eccentricity of the subject.

Don's extensive collection of home videos, newspaper clippings and fan mail, to which he has agreed to give me unlimited access, should prove to be invaluable.

Documentary Proposal – Budgie Man 1 x 23 minutes

As a young man Don Crown (aka Budgie Man) realised he had budgie power: the ability to communicate with budgies and train them to perform in magical ways. He has been busking on streets and performing with budgies for nearly half a century.

Budgie Man, the documentary, is a vibrant musical roller coaster ride through the life of Don Crown; a means of honouring the life and times of the once-dubbed 'King of the Buskers'. His energetic musical compositions will be the driving force of the film. Don's gravelly voice tones, his energy and his charisma will take us on this journey. This multi-layered documentary, with universal appeal, is bright, entertaining, compassionate and informative—a thought-provoking tale of triumph over adversity.

We open on a close-up shot of an orderly stream of budgies. The music is Don's 'I Love the Sounds of London', written when he first arrived in the city. Shots of homeless people and a variety of buskers, including Budgie Man, are juxtaposed with shots of budgies.

Cutting to Don's bedroom, it is immediately apparent that he is not a well man. He is front down, hanging over the side of his bed, coughing up phlegm—a routine he goes through every morning to clear his lungs. When Don gets up out of the bed, he sets about cleaning out his aviary. He murmurs softly to his budgies and introduces them by name.

Now sixty-two years old, Don's life has not been a bed of roses. Growing up in Durham, he left school at fifteen to begin a carpentry apprenticeship. Whilst 'eyeing up a bird', he had an industrial accident, resulting in the loss of a finger. Now unable to use the tools of his trade, he was forced to go to work down in the mines.

Tragedy struck again; in his words, "Coal dust took to my lungs." He developed the respiratory problem he still suffers from today. Major surgery ended his life as a miner.

A Teddy boy at twenty-one, he and a mate headed for London, dreaming of making it as rock stars. Lady Luck again deserted him—his mate robbed him of his life savings. He spent the next decade on the streets. "I invented living in cardboard boxes," he tells me with pride.

It is during these dark times that Don acquired his first budgie. It had been left for dead on the street, so he nursed it back to health. This was the beginning of a special relationship with budgies, which would span the rest of his life. The Budgie Man was born.

A song called 'The Police Keep Moving Me On' tells of his early years as a busker.

In footage from his collection, we see Don training the birds in his Romford garden. We see budgies riding motorbikes, flying helicopters and other diverse activities.

In 1984 he had to get rid of his budgies, as he developed an allergy to them—a source of great sorrow to him career wise, and a major spanner in the works. The next sixteen years saw the 'budgie less' Budgie Man perform with plastic budgies. Two blood transfusions in 2000 revealed that the allergy was a misdiagnosis. Comeback time for the budgies—forty of them.

Next we visit Don's garden shed-cum-recording studio, where he is recording a song, with the budgies doing the backing vocals. We are introduced to his co-writer and manager, John. We read some of the rejection letters he has received from recording companies over the years. Don gives us his take on why his music hasn't caught on.

By way of a rich tapestry of London scenes punctuated with bright shots of budgies, we listen and learn about the inspiration for his music.

'The Queen Mother's Love' was recorded and sent to Her Majesty to comfort her on the death of her mother. Don reads us a letter he received thanking him for his support in her hour of need. 'Moderation' was written for the late George Best after he had his first liver transplant. 'I Don't Like Smoke' was for an anti-smoking campaign, and was sent to the Department of Health.

Don is convinced that this song brought about the reform in smoking laws.

Music is his way of reaching out to young people, and the homeless, in an effort to spread a message of social responsibility.

Another song, 'Tony Blair's Budgie', is a satirical look at the government wasting police time.

The closing sequence is an explosion of colour as Don and his budgies perform tricks and sing his theme tune, 'I Am the Budgie Man', on the Southbank.

Johnny Lambe

NW1 PG

Hi Nick,

Thanks for being such a great bro. It was good seeing the little 'Lambies' at my fortieth birthday celebration. Glad to see you are keeping up the St Patrick's celebrations.

What courage it took to train, fight and become Hong Kong's 'Hedge Fund Fight Nite Winner 2010'. I know the pain of doing that was nothing compared to the pain in your heart.

Love you, bro.

Hong Kong's 'Fight Nite Winner 2010' (in red)

What a great fortieth birthday lunch it was with everyone dancing and singing "Go, Johnny, go."

Tess lighting the candles for Johnnys 40th

Happy 40th Birthday Johnny
'The Three Musqueteers'

Happy 40th Birthday Johnny
'The Hong Kong Fuey Leprechauns'

Glad you enjoyed our joint fortieth/seventieth birthday celebrations, Mum and Dad. The food as always was delicious. Thank you for organising it, Cheryl. Lauren, your cheesecake was a work of art.

"Cheese Cake" by Lauren Johns

Thanks for the barbecue, our Nick, and the music. Thanks, Big Nick, for providing the venue and sourcing the band; they were a delight to listen to, and they did get an enthusiastic response.

A hot day for dancing. The cheesecake was literally running off the plate, despite being protected by the marquee which we all helped to erect. The champagne and the red and white wine flowed freely into the early hours. A taxi drove up the drive just as it got dark. A memorable entrance by Hareth caused cheers and tears. Nick hoisted Hareth up on his shoulders and danced him around the floor as he would have done with me. Thank you, Nicky Mora, for stepping in quickly with comforting hugs. A good time was had by all, and we raised a large sum of money for the London Air Ambulance.

Cheers to all things country. I can hear Dolly singing 'I Will Always Love You'.

Joint Birthday Party 'Country Theme' for Johnny's 40th and John and Mona's 70th. Nick, Cheryl and Lauren

I loved the 'Jo-lympics' on 27 July in France. 'Team Nick' versus 'Team Nick'. The competition to win the prize—baskets of windfalls from the apple tree—was fierce, as was the swimming-lengths relay and the savings goals. Nick Johns was the 'sleeper', and should have been handicapped, but the tug-of-war was an epic. Lambies' team of girls and children put up a great fight, encouraged by cheers from the onlookers.

'Tug of Love Jolympics' at Monsegur on 27th July 2017

Dear Cheryl,

Thanks for all the dinners, outings, lifts and funds. When you did the Brighton Marathon, you told Mum as you were flagging a little that you saw me on my *E.T.* bike, cycling alongside you as you turned onto Hove Seafront, and it helped you over the final hard yards to the finishing line. Glad to have been there with you, Cheryl. Keep on running and fighting. Nice photo of your beret, big sis.

Cheryl and Johnny

Mummy Cheryl has finished the Brighton Marathon

Cheryl and Stu at finishing line 'You did it Cheryl'

At family get-togethers the conversation has often centred around 'Desert Island Discs'. What would you like to take with you or how would you like to be remembered?

I'd like to take, together with the Bible, *The Complete Works of Shakespeare*, the complete Roald Dahl collection and the complete J.R.R. Tolkien collection.

Johnny's Grown Up Books

Johnny's Childhood Books

I would enjoy having the time to re-read these favourites of mine. Oh yes! An atlas too, please, so that I can go virtual globetrotting; a mobile phone with an eternal battery, so that I can take wildlife photographs, listen to Classic FM, watch musicals and keep up to date with the world of films; and TWO cookery books (Trish Deseine's *Home Recipes from Ireland* and David Thompson's *Thai Food*).

My Luxury? A multi-purpose hat which can protect me from the heat in summer and the cold in winter.

My Music? If I had to pick two records, they would be *The Goonies* and *Aeroplane Over the Sea*.

How would I like to be remembered? A loving brother and son; a funny, loyal, helpful friend; a great cook; a lover of life; and a film-maker (I wish I'd had the time to make more).

Johnny's Treasures

Johnny Lambe Filmmaker with Sister Lauren

Johnny Filming

Brighton Film School. Jack Cardiff came to Visit and the write up appeared in the Evening Argos

By the way, I had a little painting hidden away which I knew Mum, or more likely Dad, would find, as he is always good on the lost-property search. A little thank-you present. I'll call it *Sea Fever*. You can look at this while you are reading Masefield's poem and hear me say, "I must go down to the sea again."

Water Colour of Boats on a River by J.W. Lambe
A Surprise for Mum and Dad which John Found recently.

Always after we'd been watching *Little House on the Prairie*, we'd echo their goodnight calls to each other when we got into bed.

"Goodnight, Mum."

"Goodnight, Jonathan."

"Goodnight, Dad."

"Goodnight, Jonboy."

"Goodnight, Cheryl."

"Goodnight, Johnny."

"Goodnight, Lauren."

"Goodnight, Johnny."

"Goodnight, Nick."

"Goodnight, Jonboy."

Goodnight All. I love you.

Who? Where? When?
How many people and places can you identify?

Johnny Howbe

XXX

each X means a million !!

Postscript
The Kid Stays in The Picture by Robert Evans

Grieving is not for sissies. It is a battle in an unending war where closure is not an option. You may have gauged from this book that grieving is an individual's battle, and each person chooses to fight the grief battle differently. Some do it by overeating, overindulgence in the grog, over-exercising, going into hibernation or partying 24/7—lots of obsessive-compulsive behaviour accompanied by outbursts of rage and resentment, even hatred, and all compounded by a lack of sleep, feelings of guilt and feelings of total inadequacy and failure. Sudden attacks of physical pain and the emotional roundabout of tears, talk and laughter all arrive unbidden. A piece of music triggers a memory, and tears roll down the cheeks, or as the Harry Bellafonte song says, 'Water come to me eye'. It may be Pavarotti singing 'Nessun Dorma', James singing 'Sit Down Next to Me', Pulp's 'Common People' or Sinead O'Connor's 'Nothing Compares to You'.

The fleeting glimpse of a 'lookee-likee' in the street, which makes your heart leap and your arms outstretch to touch; then the collapse of despair that comes with the realisation that it is not the one you've lost. I call this the 'magic roundabout of grief' which we must ride individually.

You will have read how five people in my family did it differently: Cheryl and Nick went down the physical route; Lauren, writing and painting; and you all know how Mona coped. John's 'grief journey' could be seen as typical of a man of his generation, and is perhaps the most difficult of all: suffering in silence—the stoical Ulsterman.

We must grieve to heal, as a French friend, Suzy, said: *"Mona, il faut faire ton deuil—you have to mourn."*

It is hard to believe, but the battle does get easier with time and with help from loving friends, like Helen, Mona, Angela, David, Hareth and my son-in-law, Nick Johns, who was a veritable tower of strength coming to prevent me setting the house on fire when I closed the glass lid of the hob without extinguishing the burners in the middle of a sleepless night.

After four years of trying to do it alone, I asked my doctor for help. I was given access to counselling and CBT, which was a lifeline provided by the NHS's Aldrington Centre, Hove. The young counsellor said to me, "Is there anything you'd really like to do"?

"Well," I replied, "I'd just started to write some little stories. Johnny said he'd like to help me with editing, etc., but my confidence has gone."

"Do it," she said. "It is just for you."

I did it, and *Yintin Tales* was born.

From the CBT, I learnt to recognise the triggers for my grief attacks and take some action to divert it: a walk, a coffee with a friend, etc. CBT made me aware that there are so many people out there feeling the same way.

Eventually, the paralysing attacks of pain came intermittently, thus allowing all the beautiful memories to return.

Once again, but never with the abandon of before, we dance, sing, laugh and celebrate the good times.

The empty chair will always be empty, but to quote Robert Evans, "The kid stays in the picture."

Johnny is always there for a little chat, getting up to mischief and helping us celebrate births, deaths, marriages and birthdays; and at Christmas, Easter, holidays and high days, I often sense Johnny's presence.

Sometimes on a bright sunny day, with that baby-blue sky and a soft wind blowing, I look up at what Lauren calls the 'Johnny clouds'. I listen and I can hear Johnny whisper "Life is beautiful".

Far away in the distance I hear the gentle strains of a violin as Johnny plays 'The Londonderry Air'. Do try this; I'm sure you'll hear it too.

M. Lambe, 14 February 2020

Looking Back Over My Shoulder J.W. Lambe BA (Hons)

Jonathan William Lambe
19 March 1977 to 27 July 2008

"Tomorrow will be a good day." (Captain Tom)

Acknowledgements

Thank you to the Neurological Unit of The Royal London Hospital ………

Thank you to the night nurse for making a " Palm Print ". It was inspired suggestion and I can still feel Johnny's hand in mine when I touch it.

Thanks also, to the taxi driver who picked us up at a deserted London Bridge Station on 26th July, 2007 at about six o'clock. He refused to accept payment. "This one is on me, I can see you've got trouble." This act of kindness penetrated our numbed hearts.

Thank you Maude, Michel, Vero and Laurent for organising our flight to London.

Thank you Mona and Bill and Irene and Peter.

To all of you, who have supported us through this most appalling pain.

I think, you must have found the weight and intensity of my grief exhausting. 'a burden shared is a burden halved'. My friend Helen Nelson never failed to listen and give words of hope and comfort. Some find this unburdening too painful and feel it should be left to the professionals. After four years I went to my GP and said "I NEED HELP". He immediately organised one-to-one Bereavement Counselling. I found this excellent and it prepared me for CBT in a small group, where I was able to hear about many situations which cause mental health problems from others in the group. The piece of advice I most value came after a question from the counsellor.

"Is there anything in your life you'd really like to do?"

"I'd like to finish writing the short stories Johnny was going to edit for me."

"DO IT "was the response! "DO IT FOR YOU."

My therapy was "Yintin Tales". It allowed me to go back to a very happy place and gave me time to heal. A very special thank you to the N.H.S., the staff at the Aldrington Centre in Hove and my GP Dr. Bird for the referral.

A very special thank you to our life long friends, Angela and David Duffin. Two of the most generous, patient, loving, loyal people in the world. We have laughed cried, argued and holidayed together for over fifty years and Johnny has a very special place in their hearts. Also thanks to Nicola Duffin (the God Daughter).

Love you A. and D. and N. xx

John, aka Buster and Mona

Thank you Helen Clifford Ringwood for the Golden Angel.

Thank you Hareth Pochee ' friend extraordinaire'.

Thank you to Pamela and Ben for your generous lunch at the GINGER PIG.

Thank you to the team at KILLER CREATIVE you did a great job at very short notice.

Thank you Ruari White for giving up your time to help me.

Thank you Finn White our computer whiz.

Thank you Lauren and Cheryl my two best girls and go to people.

Thank you Nick so proud of my son. I love the Tattoo of Johnny, tucked safely under your arm.

Thank you Trish Colley (was Harris) for inscribing "Book of Memories".

Thank you to the London Air Ambulance Service. Your swift response enabled us to spend one last night with our son.

Thank you Bertie Jenkins for the Beachcombing Pictures of Johnny in the West of Ireland.

Thank you Brian and Josephine Mehaffey for the photo of Johnny, *"Food and Love"* taken at the 'Big Christening' in Stamford circa '87. One of the million kisses he either gave or sent to me.

Thank you to Miles Bailey of The Choir Press for his patience, empathy and professionalism. He has been "A Man for All Seasons".

Finally thank you to my beautiful Johnny.

I miss you.

Mum

21st June, 2020

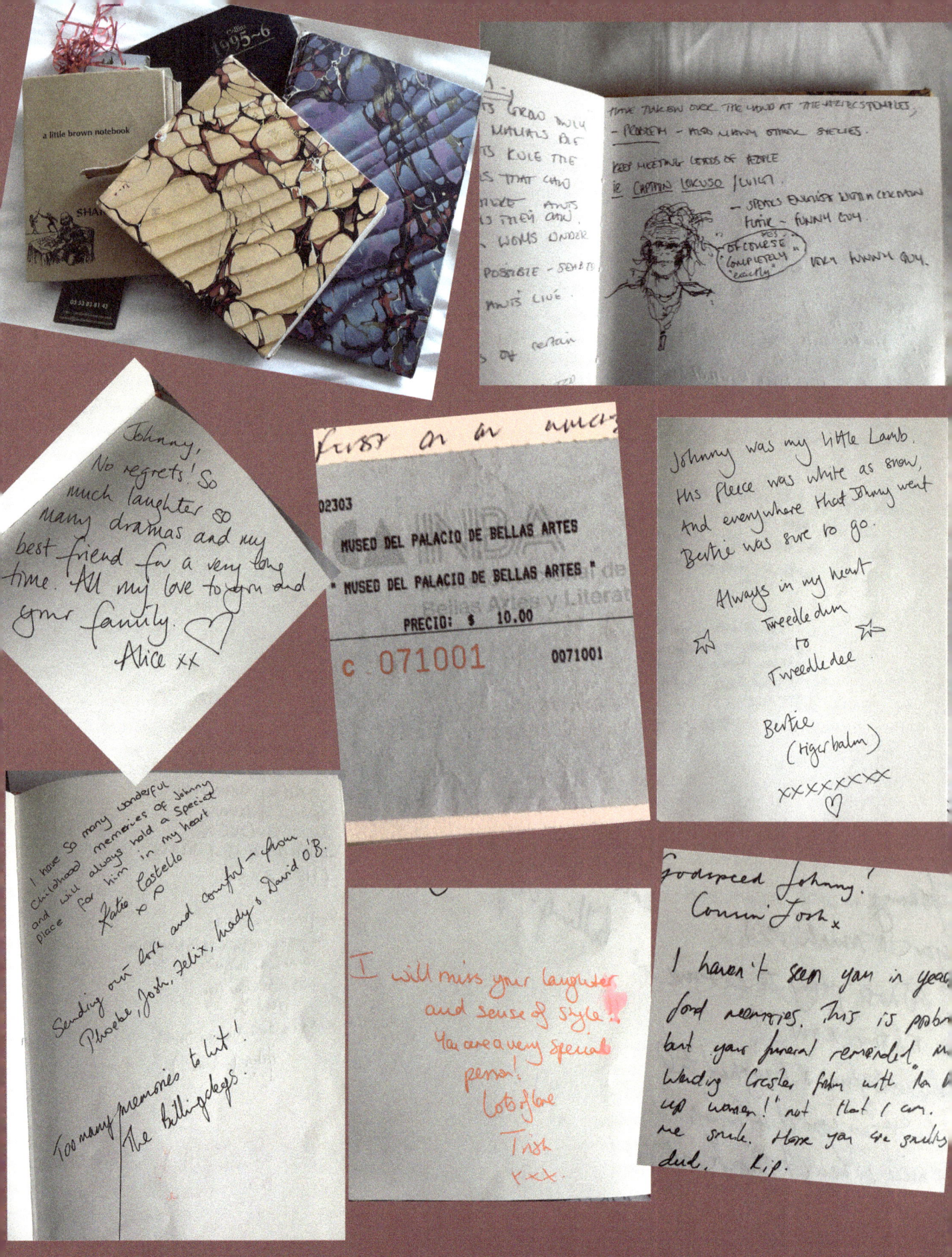

www.ingramcontent.com/pod-product-compliance
Ingram Content Group UK Ltd.
Pitfield, Milton Keynes, MK11 3LW, UK
UKHW052120230426
12049UKWH00009BA/138